GHOSTS AND LEGENDS OF MICHIGAN'S WEST COAST

D1596631

GHOSTS AND LEGENDS OF MICHIGAN'S WEST COAST

AMBERROSE HAMMOND

Haunted America

Published by Haunted America
A Division of The History Press
Charleston, SC 29403
www.historypress.net

Copyright © 2009 by Amberrose Hammond
All rights reserved

First published 2009
Second printing 2010
Third printing 2012
Fourth printing 2013

Manufactured in the United States

ISBN 978.1.59629.663.3

Library of Congress Cataloging-in-Publication Data

Hammond, Amberrose.
Ghosts and legends of Michigan's west coast / Amberrose Hammond.
p. cm.
Includes bibliographical references and index.
ISBN 978-1-59629-663-3 (alk. paper)
1. Ghosts--Michigan. 2. Haunted places--Michigan. I. Title.
BF1472.U6H355 2009
133.109774--dc22
2009026269

This book is dedicated to Michigan's paranormal world and the people who explore it. May it continue to create awe and inspiration, always leaving us with the feeling that there's something "extra" going on in our little, mundane world.

CONTENTS

ACKNOWLEDGEMENTS

I would like to thank The History Press for giving me the opportunity to write my first book on a topic I have loved since I was a kid; Tom Maat, my partner in crime, for all of his help, support, driving, pictures and late-night "rumrunners" at the Tip; Jeanette Weiden in the local history/genealogy department and the rest of my helpful co-workers at Loutit District Library for helping me find old, forgotten information; Troy Taylor and Rosemary Ellen Guiley for inspiring me years ago with their wonderful books; Julie Williams for listening to me go on…and on and on; my buddy Jason Gowin for reminding me that if I didn't do certain things, I "wouldn't be Amber"; my friends and family for putting up with and supporting my crazy ghost-hunting ways; and lastly, Ghostly Talk Paranormal Radio out of Warren, Michigan, and its co-ghost and my better half, Scott Lambert, for their continued efforts to bring quality information to the paranormal world.

INTRODUCTION

What if there really are ghosts in this world? What if there are grains of truth hiding within the stories and legends? This is what keeps many, if not most of us, on a search for the unknown, the spooky and the strange, especially if it's close to home. You probably have that urge yourself, hence the reason you picked up this very book! Ghosts have inspired people throughout the ages. From creepy tales told around a campfire on a summer's night to great authors like Edgar Allan Poe and even Shakespeare, there's no doubt that ghost stories are a part of our world and are here to stay. For some, they are just entertaining stories, but for others, they are very real experiences. There are hundreds of thousands of events that normal people have experienced that can't be explained. We can't deny that there is something in this world beyond our normal senses.

Whether you call Michigan's west coast home or are just a passing tourist enjoying our coastal beaches and unique sand dunes, you should know that Michigan isn't short of ghost stories and legends. Tales of spectral ships, haunted lighthouses, unexplained creatures and ghosts walking among the living are all part of Michigan's rich ghost lore. The tales in this book are written as I have learned them or as they have been told to me. No doubt, there are slight variations of each. I have been studying and investigating Michigan's paranormal world since 2000, and collected here are some of my favorite stories about Michigan's west coast. Some stories are well over one hundred years old, and a few are new ghost stories in the making. Some of the tales in this book involve my own personal experiences with the paranormal through investigations and talking with all kinds of people about their supernatural experiences.

Ghosts and legends are a fun part of what makes us human. When we don't understand something, we tend to create a story to help explain it. Many ghost stories and legends come from unexplainable and mysterious events that become stories and are passed down through generations. Native Americans used legends to illuminate the hidden world around them and how it operated. These tales taught lessons and had meaning. Our modern-day ghost stories have meaning as well. They give us hope that there is something beyond our physical plane of existence, and they keep a little bit of wonder in our thoughts. A ghost story told at night takes us back to a time when the home was lit with oil lamps and the nights were darker than dark, not polluted by the light of nearby cities. So wait until night to pick up this book, grab a flashlight and throw a blanket over your head (it doesn't matter if you're all grown up)—and better yet, wait for a stormy night. Happy Hauntings!

THE GHOST OF THE GRAND THEATRE

Sometimes work is the only thing people know. Their jobs become their lives, and in the case of John Buchanan, former custodian of the old Grand Theatre in Grand Haven, it became an afterlife as well. Many believe that John haunted the building when it was up and running as a movie theatre and maybe continues to do so to this day.

The Grand Theatre opened its doors on January 23, 1928, at a time when motion pictures were just starting to become popular. Vaudeville shows were still traveling the nation, and the word "Hollywood" was fresh to the ears. The Grand Theatre stage was equipped for plays and traveling shows, complete with dressing rooms behind the stage and in the basement. Traveling troupes and even the old "freak shows" entertained the people of Grand Haven, and from those old vaudeville troupes, the first rumors of ghosts in the dark corners of the building started to surface.

The original L-shaped theatre was built for about $380,000 and was inspired by Italian design, with its stucco roof and ornate tile work on the front lobby roof. The theatre boasted 833 seats for filmgoers. Frank Fisher was a longtime manager of the Grand for over twenty years from the 1940s to the 1960s. Having been on the vaudeville circuit with his wife for many years, Frank knew many of the actors who were appearing in the movies of his time and was able to bring a little bit of Hollywood to Grand Haven.

Many decades later, the 1990s brought about the dawn of the multi-screen theatre, and it became difficult for a single-screen movie house to compete. In 1996, Amy Lake and husband, D.T. LaVercombe, bought the theatre and hoped to do something exciting with the place, but as rumor circulated about a multi-screen theatre coming into Grand Haven, the end looked like it was near. The husband-and-wife duo tried to breathe life into the building one last time by getting a liquor license. They offered beer and wine with dinner during the movie, later renovating the old seating to add tables to create a dinner-and-a-movie experience. While it was a fun idea, it wasn't enough, and the pair sold the building to local businessman Steve Loftis. Many ideas bounced around about making a fine arts center or a fancy hotel out of the building, but in the end, the theatre portion of the Grand met its end with a wrecking ball to make room for high-end condominiums. It was a sad day as people poked around the rubble of the building, picking up a brick or two as souvenirs of times gone by.

Petie Oom, a lifelong resident of Grand Haven, remembers growing up and hanging out as a kid in the Grand. It was one of the places in town where she spent plenty of time, watching movies and getting into trouble. One day, Petie decided to be mischievous and write her name on a chair in the theatre. The manager, Frank Fisher, promptly kicked her out, knowing exactly who the little girl named "Petie" was. After being kicked out, Petie went around to the back of the building, and when the lights inside the theatre went dark and the movie projector beamed the image onto the screen, the custodian, John Buchanan, kindly opened the door and let Petie sneak back in to watch the movie.

Born on May 12, 1903, in Hastings, Nebraska, John Buchanan moved to Grand Haven when he was a kid. He went to Grand Haven High School and did odd jobs around town, working as a grocery store clerk for five years at City Grocery on Washington Street. When construction of the theatre began, John started working for the contractor, painting and installing seating. His hard work paid off and secured him a job as custodian of the place when it opened its doors. He worked as a custodian for thirty-nine years until he retired. He was also the custodian for the Robin Hood Theatre in town until it closed in 1951.

John became a fixture in the Grand. He would spend his entire day working, sometimes from 9:00 a.m. to 2:00 a.m., cleaning up after a late show. An interview with him printed in the *Grand Haven Tribune* on January

24, 1968, stated that he was "one of the most dedicated men you'll ever meet…probably the world's most efficient enemy of dirt." People who remember the Grand in its earlier days still remember John Buchanan. Alice Bos, a longtime resident of Grand Haven, remembers him clearly. "John would mutter and talk to himself," she said, "but was always very nice. He just seemed a little 'slow.'"

Petie Oom eventually secured a job at the theatre when she was a teenager. When she first started to work with John, she was a little frightened. He was slightly "off," as most people remembered, but as she grew to know him, she found him to be one of the most friendly guys around the place, always quick to lend a helping hand and taking care of any need the building had. Her fear of him faded fast:

> *John was always a nice guy, we even made sure to give him dinner when my mom had made a big meal. He actually lived right next door to me in an apartment house on Franklin, and when we had a big meal, my mom would send me over to his place with a hot plate of dinner for him.*

John Buchanan in 1968 at the old projector of the Grand Theatre. *Photo courtesy of the* Grand Haven Tribune.

Interestingly enough, Petie remembered that John was the one telling people ghost stories:

> *He would take me downstairs in the basement where there were all these tiny, cement dressing rooms for use back in the Vaudeville days. There was only a small overhead light bulb hanging from the ceiling and barely any light down there. I was scared just going down there. John would always tell me, "The vaudevilles are still here. If you ever hear any noises down in the basement, it's just the ghosts of the vaudevilles making noise."*

This terrified Petie so much that she wouldn't go down to the basement alone after hearing that. One might say that the "ghost of the Grand" was the first guy to start telling ghost stories about the place.

Years and years later, when the Central Park Players were hosting a play at the theatre, Petie volunteered to help with hair and makeup. Some of the people in the play were interested in the now "old" theatre, especially the basement. They no doubt had heard a few rumors of ghosts and wanted to explore the hidden parts of the building.

Petie volunteered to take them all down into the basement and show them the tiny dressing rooms that John used to show her. That same spooky feeling washed over her as they looked around the basement, and Petie and the rest of the gang turned around and went back to the safety of the stage upstairs. Was it the ghosts of those vaudevilles that spooked all them out of the basement or was good old John already haunting his favorite place in the world?

Throughout the building's history, especially starting in the 1980s, strange moments and mysterious activity couldn't be ignored. Employees experienced things that couldn't easily be explained. Former employees reported coming in one day and finding garbage bags tied up and ready to go out. No one confessed to the mysterious deed, and seeing that it was a custodian's job to take care of the garbage, people started to wonder if John was continuing his job in the theatre even though he was long dead and buried.

In addition to the ghostly cleaning, other things would happen, such as phantom footsteps heard when no one was around, lights turning on and off by themselves and the occasional glimpse of someone from the corner of the eye. It was even rumored that a grave was in the basement. There were old tunnels under downtown Grand Haven connecting many of the buildings, but most are now blocked off. In a *Grand Haven Tribune* article from 1996 reporting on the haunting, a person told how he went beneath where the old concession stand used to be and found himself in a tunnel where a mound of sand "looked like an Indian burial site." There was speculation as to whether someone had been buried down there at some point.

Sara, a former employee, recalled working there during high school from 1991 to 1994. She worked behind the concession stand, took tickets and performed other odd jobs. She remembered the feeling of always being watched and was constantly looking over her shoulder or turning her head because she would see glimpses of someone standing nearby, but no one would ever be there. On her shifts, doors would often shut and open again on the second floor. One time, a friend of hers was in the projector booth loading a movie when a white feather fell from the ceiling. It doesn't sound like much, but the booth was tiny and cramped, and she couldn't figure out where on earth the feather had come from. Could it have been from John? Sara said that everyone who worked at the Grand had some sort of experience, some more intense than others.

Emily Bruno was also a former employee and really loved working at the Grand. Emily recalled some of her spooky experiences while working there in the 1990s. Her first experience happened before she even got a job there. She was in a play taking place at the theatre, and it was her first time being on the stage. She remembers:

> *There was a staircase that went up to dressing rooms and everything was very gothic, old and elaborate looking. Very pretty. We would sometimes wander up there when we weren't busy with other things, and I always felt a shift in the environment. Things were different back there. Boxes backstage seemed to shift on their own while I was there, and I felt like I was being watched. Before we had ever even heard about John, we had made up our minds that the place was haunted!*

When Emily got a job there, other parts of the building gave her the same creepy feeling that she had experienced when she first explored the backstage area. Emily remembered the janitor's closet, no doubt John's closet at one point:

> *I hated going in there alone. I never felt threatened or anything but it was dark and old and I was fourteen. We would argue over who had to go and get the mop. We hated changing the mop water just because that meant more time in the janitor closet. I don't think there was one person working there who didn't have some sort of experience.*

Emily had also heard that the old projector room had a "life of its own." Some of the people who worked in there experienced strange occurrences as well, such as the mysterious feather that appeared out of nowhere.

After noticing one too many strange happenings, Emily finally said something to her boss, and that's when she was told the stories about John. Emily remembered that her boss would sometimes say things to John if she sensed him around and his "activities" would change. If her boss said, "I'm busy right now John," whatever was happening would stop. After Emily heard the stories about John, she lost the uneasy feeling she got when something didn't feel quite right. "It was actually kind of nice sensing him around. I never did get comfortable with those dressing rooms though. I don't know what that was about, but perhaps it was because I was so young at the time."

Mike Naramore was a former manager during the Grand's last days as a cinema. When asked about the haunting, Mike stated:

> *I'm very familiar with the ghost of John, who was the old custodian of the theatre when it opened. I never saw any apparitions, but there were some extremely anomalous noises, drafts and strange electrical fields we encountered while working there. We usually attributed them all to John, however tongue-in-cheek it might have been.*

As of 2006, the only part of the original Grand Theatre still standing is the front lobby, which is a restaurant called the Theatre Bar. Developers tore down the actual theatre for condos. It was a real shame to see the beautiful place torn down. Perhaps diners will find themselves sharing a meal with a custodial ghost, or maybe John decided to move on after his beloved theatre was torn down.

The Ghost of the Grand Theatre

The old, beautiful lobby of the Grand Theatre. This portion is now the Theatre Bar. *Photo courtesy of the* Grand Haven Tribune.

A *Grand Haven Tribune* article from 1968 stated:

> *The Grand is more than a building to* [John]—*it's alive with all kinds of memories—a changing world on film—a sea of friendly faces of patrons who call him by the first name,* [and] *John almost has a reverence for the Grand—A respect only a sincere workman can acquire.*

So as you pass the old front entrance to the one-time theatre, say hello to John, as he might still be there. Only now he's enjoying fine dining and sushi rather than old movies. Let's hope that he's grabbed a table and put his feet up for a while rather than toiling away on the other side.

THE LEGEND
OF THE MELON HEADS

Imagine it is a warm summer's night in the area that is now the Saugatuck State Park in the 1970s. A teenage couple drive their car down what used to be a dirt road and put it into park to get more "acquainted" with each other. The hormones start to fly, and the outside world becomes a blur…until a tiny knock is heard on the passenger's side window. The couple unlock their lips and look toward the window, expecting to see an officer telling them to move on. Instead, they see a childlike, large-headed creature staring back at them, its nose just touching the bottom of the car window. The whites of its eyes are all they can see, as the irises seem to be at the bottom of the eyelid. The frightened couple scream in unison; the boy starts the car, shifts it into drive and they peel out of the park at high speeds, wondering what sort of monster they have just encountered. To this day, sightings of what have become known as the Melon Heads continue to circulate in the cities of Holland and Saugatuck.

According to the legend, there used to be a hospital in the area that treated children with a condition known as hydrocephalus, which causes the head to swell to large proportions. The doctor treating the children would experiment on the unfortunate souls until they were barely able to function. When the hospital closed down, the children were released and left to fend for themselves. Many say that they banded together in the woods around the Saugatuck State Park area, where they still live to this day.

The Legend of the Melon Heads

Not only are the Melon Heads purported to live in west Michigan, but they also have some distant cousins in northern Ohio. The stories that come from Ohio tell of feral, vicious little creatures that will kill your dog, attack and potentially eat you or run alongside your car at cheetah-like speeds. This Ohio variety seems to be a little more dangerous than our Michigan brand of Melon Heads. The Ohio legend has many slight variations of the same story that involve a Dr. Crowe who was a cruel and sadistic man. The Ohio version says that he ran a hospital in the late 1800s to help hydrocephalic children. Instead of treating them, he tortured the helpless victims by injecting more fluid into their brains and conducting other experiments on them, eventually leaving them on

An old tintype of a mother with a hydrocephalic child. *Photo courtesy of the Thanatos Archive.*

their own. The stories are nearly identical, but there is no evidence of a hospital in the Saugatuck area that ever treated this condition or of a doctor who specifically housed and tended to children suffering from hydrocephalus. It's not known which version came first, but it is obvious that the two are related somehow.

Unlike the uncertainty of the Melon Heads' existence, hydrocephalus is a very real condition. About one in five hundred children are affected by hydrocephalus, or "water on the brain." The cerebrospinal fluid in the brain doesn't drain properly, and the result is an enlarged head, with a normal-sized face and features. It is especially noticeable in infants and children under the age of three because the spinal plates have yet to fuse; the head becomes very large since the skull is still able to expand, unlike in adults and older children, whose plates have already fused. The eyes of the children also have a downward gaze, as the pressure caused from the buildup of fluid in the head makes the irises look down, exposing the whites of the eyes as if they were zombies. Although it is a very sad condition, hydrocephalous can result in a very disturbing image, one that could easily give birth to legend. But how did this story ever get started? Was their a doctor in the area testing children?

Our logical sides tell us that there is no way a band of small children would be living in the wilds of the Saugatuck State Park, completely feral and ready to lash out at any person who happens their way. But our curious sides wonder. What if there were a couple of kids left on the side of the road like abandoned kittens who lived in the woods for a while? The story had to come from somewhere, right? There has to be some grain of truth in it somewhere…

One possible theory is that this story got its roots back in the early 1900s. The Forward Movement Settlement was a charitable organization out of Chicago in the early twentieth century. It owned 130 acres of beautiful Saugatuck lakeshore that it called the Forward Movement Park. One of the services it offered was the Vesta Putnam Summer School for Crippled Children. One can only imagine that in an area of vacationers and people with money, just as today, the kids of the day probably made fun of the children from the school. Stories started, and maybe the school even had a few hydrocephalic students. It's just a theory, but a very probable one considering that the school was in the same area where the legend started.

The Legend of the Melon Heads

Even though the story's origins aren't clear, this popular Holland-area legend has been around for well over fifty years, told and retold by teenagers, popular at every Halloween and used by parents as leverage to get their kids to go to sleep on time. Tom Maat of Michigan's Otherside remembers telling his children in the 1970s to "go to bed or the Melon Heads will come for you!" The kids promptly went to bed, fearing a visit from bulbous-headed children seeking vengeance for their ill-treated lives.

Over the years, the legend has become entangled with other local legends in the area, such as the Felt Mansion and the old minimum-security jail that used to stand behind the mansion when it was the state police post. Some like to say that the Melon Heads lived in the jail and that's where they were experimented on; others have gone so far as to say that they lived at the Felt Mansion. Both rumors are historically untrue. The Junction Insane Asylum, a mythical place talked about for years, has also been thrown into the mix in recent years thanks to websites and urban legends that spread as fast as a ghost disappears. Some have called the jail behind the Felt Mansion "the Junction," claiming that the Melon Heads were born there. According to the Allegan County Historical Society, there are no historical records or any documentation of any kind supporting the existence of the Junction Insane Asylum. It is pure legend. With all these urban legends floating about, stories can often start to meld when there are more than a few stories coming out of one location, and that seems to be the case with the Melon Heads.

Tom Maat grew up and spent his youth in the Holland/Saugatuck area and remembers first hearing about the Melon Heads more than thirty-five years ago when he was sixteen years old:

> *Just before you got to the Felt Mansion, the Melon Heads lived on top of a big hill in the area. The hill had a stairway going up it and a windmill sat on top and supplied water to the nearby Felt Mansion when it was a seminary. The area was a popular make-out spot because it was in the middle of nowhere then. People said the Melon Heads would roam around those woods at night.*

Tom remembers that the Melon Heads were said to come from a nearby hospital that never really existed. But what has continued to perpetuate this legend if there is absolutely no basis of truth in it? Could it have something to do with a reel-to-reel? As teenagers, bored and armed with a battery-operated reel-to-reel complete with creepy sounds recorded on it, Tom Maat and his friends would hide out in the dark woods of the Saugatuck State Park, waiting for cars to pull up and turn off their lights. The unsuspecting couple in the car making out weren't ready for the eerie sounds floating out of the nearby woods. Most likely, the couple would freeze up, question each other about the noises and hesitate to look outside into the inky black surroundings.

"Did you hear something?"

"No…did you hear something?"

The couple would start to turn their heads to look out the window. At the right moment, Tom and his buddies would come tearing out of the woods and bang on the car windows, causing the terrified couple to flee the parking lot in a frenzy of squealing tires and dust. Surprisingly, Tom noted that they never got their butts kicked to Lake Michigan and back. And for all we know, those couples Tom and his band of merry "Melon Heads" terrified are the ones still telling people to this day that the Melon Heads are out there, waiting to pounce on unsuspecting cars.

Is there any truth behind this legend? Maybe not. But do you care to drive your car into the territory of the Melon Heads on a moonless night? Maybe as you cuddle up to your sweetheart, you just might find yourself being stared at by a bulbous-headed creature, or it might just be Tom, thirty-five years later, still hanging out with his now vintage reel-to-reel, playing scary sounds from the woods. So keep your dogs on a leash, steer your children away from the woods of the Melon Heads and keep an eye peeled for a big-headed creature running alongside your car. And if you do see one, please try to stay calm so that you can at least get one good photo for posterity. After the photo is shot, feel free to start screaming.

THE SHOE TREE LEGEND

Coming upon a shoe tree can be a strange and shocking experience, especially if you've never seen one before. Shoe trees are usually big old trees with branches resembling arthritic fingers reaching up from the ground. They are sometimes found in remote locations but are more often located on busy roads, such as the supposed "original" shoe tree in Kalkaska on Highway 131 going north. This tree has hundreds of pairs of shoes dangling from its limbs like bizarre Christmas ornaments. Known as folk art, or just roadside oddities, around the United States, the legend of the shoe trees in Michigan have a more sinister origin.

The legend says that shoe trees started with one tree in Walled Lake, found with many tiny children's shoes dangling from its branches. When the tree was found in the woods, the disappearance of children who had been missing was solved: they had all been murdered. The man behind the murders was dubbed the "Walled Lake child killer." He was from the Novi area and had an evil urge to kill innocent children. After he took their lives, he took their shoes, tied them together at the laces and tossed them up in the tree. The shoes dangled back and forth until they hung motionless, a metaphor for all of the young lives he carelessly snuffed. Supposedly, the shoe tree was on Thirteen Mile Road, and the sounds of the crying children could be heard at night as their ghosts searched for their mothers. From that point on, people visited the shoe tree and threw their own pairs of shoes into the limbs as a memorial to the children who were killed.

But is there any evidence behind this legend at all? Was there really a Walled Lake child killer? Do people have paranormal experiences near

The "original" shoe tree in Kalkaska along Highway 131 North. *Photo by Stacy Carroll.*

shoe trees? It is likely that the legend itself makes people believe there is something paranormal going on with shoe trees. For the most part, shoe trees are just a fun form of art, but there's something disturbing about all those shoes hanging from the branches and the energy left behind from all of the different people who walked to so many places in each pair. There are stories about kids daring each other to approach a shoe tree and toss a pair up or take a pair in the middle of the night. The shoe tree in Kalkaska has been there for years and years, and no one is certain who put the first pair of shoes in the tree or for what reason, but hundreds of other people have followed suit through the years.

After being flooded with requests for information about the Walled Lake child killer, the Walled Lake Library issued a statement in 2005 on the urban legend. It felt that the story of the killer and his shoe tree might have been inspired by four murdered children from Oakland County in 1976 and 1977. The murders went unsolved. The bodies were found in Franklin Village, Livonia, Southfield and Troy, but nowhere near Walled Lake. Some speculate that a tiny pair of antique kid's shoes found in a tree in the area was the inspiration for the popular urban legend.

Murderers and dead children aside, there is a lighter side to the shoe trees scattered across the state. Upon seeing these trees, many get the urge to add their own shoes to the branches. Some say that the shoe trees are there to provide shoes to people who need them. Old shoes disappear and new ones appear all the time. The website *Roadside America* writes that if you "knock a pair of shoes off a shoe tree…you will be cursed," as each pair of shoes still harnesses the energy of its previous owner.

No doubt shoe trees will continue to pop up over the state from time to time, and old ones will continue to grow with shoes, not leaves. New stories will start with each new tree. When you drive past the Kalkaska shoe tree, make sure to bring a pair of old shoes with you. Tie the shoelaces together good and tight, wind your arm back and give a good throw. If your shoes make it on the first toss, make a wish and it's sure to come true—just don't knock another pair off!

HAUNTED LAKE FOREST CEMETERY

By day, this sprawling, historical cemetery makes for a pleasant walk for any graveyard enthusiast, but by night, some feel that the cemetery comes alive with spirits and glowing figures that prowl the grounds, guarding their tombstones and fellow cemetery residents. It has become a popular spot for paranormal enthusiasts to investigate while visiting Grand Haven.

EARLY HISTORY OF LAKE FOREST

Our Village has grown; our graveyard now is in our very midst—the dead and living being in too close proximity for our own ideas of comfort.
—Grand Haven News, *1859*

History and hauntings walk hand in hand. Without the history, there is no haunting. It seems that there has to be an event in the past, whether traumatic or life altering in some fashion, that creates a haunted place or a ghost. The history of Lake Forest Cemetery is a fascinating one and perhaps gives clues as to why a few of its deceased residents continue living past their earthly expiration dates.

Early Grand Haven was a bustling and rapidly expanding village when it started. Established along the Grand River and on Lake Michigan, the town became an important port for the shipping industry with big cities such as Chicago and Milwaukee. Grand Haven's downtown area continued to expand until businesses and homes started to come face to face with the dead living among them.

The first municipal cemetery was originally planned out by pioneer and fur trader Rix Robinson. Robinson owned the original deed to the land in the Grand Haven area and set off a chunk of it for a cemetery in the region that is now Central Park. This area was once surrounded by woods, but as the years went on, the city expanded and was soon bumping heads with the graveyard. Death wasn't something that people wanted to be reminded about on a daily basis. A dilapidated fence decayed around the cemetery, and cows haphazardly grazed on the graveyard grass. The cemetery was also becoming a health issue. Many of the deceased buried there had died of such diseases as tuberculosis and blackwater fever, a form of malaria. Grand Haven historian Wallace Ewing noted in his *Directory of Places in Northwest Ottawa County* that "fears began to rise that the bodies in the old cemetery were giving off 'miasmas,' noxious vapors that were believed to seep from corpses."

In 1883, the city council passed a resolution to move the graveyard to a more suitable place. Before the resolution, land had been purchased on the outskirts of the town in 1862 with the intention of creating the new Lake Forest Cemetery. The new burial grounds would be keeping up with the emerging idea of a "garden cemetery," a concept that was happening all over the United States. Garden cemeteries were peaceful places with benches for sitting and pathways to walk along while visiting deceased loved ones—something far different from the crowded, unsanitary and neglected graveyards of the past. Needing a special place for Grand Haven's pioneers, Ferry Hill was established on Lake Forests' highest point, and the bodies were moved from the Central Park cemetery and buried on the hill. It was the request of the Ferry family that their dead relatives and friends be buried together in a special area.

While the founders' bodies were moved first, moving the rest of the Central Park burials did not happen at a fast rate. To encourage body removal, the city came up with a plan. Imagine the lack of enthusiasm among Grand Havenites when they were told to move the dead on their own in exchange for a free burial plot in the new cemetery. It was probably not a task that a lot of people jumped at right away. And what of the people whose friends and family had moved out of the area or were long gone themselves? They were probably the people who were unexpectedly dug up when work began to turn the old, dilapidated city cemetery into a fresh and enjoyable park years later.

Local historian Bob Beaton spent a considerable amount of time researching and reading old *Grand Haven Tribune* articles, and in his booklet on the history of Central Park and its fountain, *Tribune* articles from 1900 tell how, "in plowing today, they came across the brick foundation of what was probably once a vault in the old cemetery that used to be located there. Several human bones were also found." Another article read:

> *A human skeleton was found this afternoon by the city employees at work grading the city park. The bones were gathered together and it was suggested that they be cleaned and taken by the school. On the skull was found considerable hair of reddish color, despite the fact that the body had been buried 25 years. It is believed that still more skeletons will be found.*

The article mentions a pocketbook with one cent found near the skeleton. The coin was from 1865, giving a clue as to when the person was buried. It can be safely assumed that a few people are still buried in the park where weddings take place every year and where people go to read and enjoy a patch of sunshine spilling onto the lawn through the trees. Do spirits of that long-ago cemetery still linger around the little park today?

THE BLUE MAN LEGEND OF LAKE FOREST CEMETERY

A group of people gather on Ferry Hill in Lake Forest Cemetery. It is a clear night, and the moon above casts just enough light to give the small burial ground of Grand Haven's founders an unearthly glow. The wind rustles through trees surrounding the graves. A crow is heard in the distance, sounding the midnight hour. Everyone's eyes are darting around, watching dark shadows move about and wondering if it's just their vision playing tricks on them or the restless spirits of the cemetery moving about.

"What's that?" says a girl in the group in a frightened whisper. The group looks in the direction of her pointed finger at the tomb of William M. Ferry. A blue glow is forming above it in the shape of a person. The adventurous group is petrified, and no one can move a muscle. They watch as the blue form slowly fades back into the night, and when the misty substance is completely gone, everyone takes off running at speeds they never thought achievable. Had the group of curiosity seekers just experienced the Blue Man of Lake Forest Cemetery?

For ages, kids and adults have been telling stories about a mysterious "blue light" and "Blue Man" in Lake Forest Cemetery. In the late 1960s, high school students talked about the light. During an interview with a Grand Haven resident who was in school in the late '60s, he remembered being in the cemetery one night and seeing a blue light that seemingly came from nowhere. Was that the start of the legend? He stated that he didn't know what it was or where it came from, only that they all remember seeing a blue light dancing around in the surrounding woods of the cemetery.

In the 1970s, high school students continued to talk about the blue light, only now it became the blue light of Duncan's Woods. Duncan's Woods is an area of old-growth forest donated to Grand Haven by the Duncan family. Duncan's Woods borders the Lake Forest property and when the Duncans passed on, their bodies were buried near their beautiful woods. Eventually, kids started to talk of a strange blue light coming from the Duncans' tombstones. At that time, the Duncans' plot was very secluded and private and set apart from other monuments, making it an easy target for graveyard stories.

With the arrival of the 1980s, the tale took another turn, and this seems to be the beginning of the Blue Man. The story, for the most part, has stayed the same since then. The Blue Man is reportedly seen atop Ferry Hill, also known as Founder's Hill. Ferry Hill's special significance lies in the fact that it is the final resting place of Grand Haven's early pioneers. People who have claimed to see this spectral shade say that the entity is a hazy blue color standing near the Reverend William M. Ferry's grave. Nothing malicious is felt about this glowing spirit, but many like to speculate that it is the soul of William Ferry, also known as the "father of Grand Haven," watching over the cemetery on top of his lonely citadel. Some speculate that his spirit is restless because

The tomb of William M. Ferry in Lake Forest Cemetery. *Photo by Amberrose Hammond.*

his tomb has been desecrated in the past. It was once an aboveground vault, but the top slab was shoved off the vault sometime in the past. Heavy vandalism in the 1950s and early '80s eventually caused the city to build a protective fence around the historical plots in an attempt to thwart vandals.

But who or what is this mysterious mist that haunts Ferry Hill? Is it even real? Has anyone ever really seen it?

THE MAN BEHIND THE GHOST

Reverend William Montegue Ferry and his family came to Grand Haven in 1834 after running a mission school on Mackinaw Island. Born in Granby, Massachusetts, in 1796, Ferry became a Presbyterian minister at the age of twenty-six in 1822. He was described in history books as a man of medium height, quiet, a good listener and a simple man who didn't flaunt the money he acquired later in life.

William Ferry and his wife, Amanda, started their mission school on Mackinaw Island in 1823 for the local Native Americans, namely métis children of the fur trade society. *Métis* refers to the mixed children of different Native American tribes and European or French-Canadian men. Many of the métis children who lived in the Lake Superior region were sent to the Ferry school on Mackinaw to get a "European education." The children always seemed stuck in the middle, learning Native American traditions from their mothers and learning European ways in school and from their fathers.

Old history books on Grand Haven portray the Reverend Ferry as a "saint-like" figure and a father of a successful town, but some historians don't agree with that portrayal. Ferry and his wife were Evangelical Protestants. People then and today don't agree with how the Native Americans were forced to become "Americanized," further exposing them to prejudice and a feeling of inferiority along with forcing them to accept a new religion. According to author Keith R. Widden in his book *Battle for the Soul*, "The work of the missionaries at Mackinac

Reverend William Montague Ferry. *Photo courtesy of the Loutit District Library.*

coincide with the effort by the United States government, its agents, and its citizens to incorporate what remained of the Northwest Territory into the United States." The métis children were part of the fur trade society. American businessmen had money tied into the fur trade, and it was in their best interest to bring the fur trade society to the white man's idea of the world and its ways. The Ferrys' efforts to "save" the souls of the Native American children and change their way of life hasn't always been looked at in a favored light by everyone. Evangelical Protestantism was new at the time, as well, and was looked at with a suspicious eye.

When Ferry's mission work came to an end on Mackinaw Island, it was time to find a new business venture elsewhere. Lumber was big, so Ferry took a daunting trip in a canoe with two Native American guides down the coast of Lake Michigan, scouting the area for good lumber and a place to live. The following year, Ferry and his friend Pierre Duvernay hiked from Detroit to the Grand River and sailed down the Grand in a canoe until they reached the mouth of the river, which is the site of Grand Haven today. The land that Ferry decided to settle on was actually deeded to Rix Robinson, a man who for sometime had a trading post in Grand Haven and a four-room house. Ferry went into business with Robinson, and some of Robinson's land was split up to create the start of Grand Haven. The first twenty-one people to start their lives in Grand Haven arrived on November 2, 1834, by boat. William Ferry's home was the first permanent settlement in Grand Haven, along with a church. His home sat on the corner of Harbor and Washington Streets, where the Kirby Grill is located today, and burned down in 1866. The Kirby Grill is said to be haunted.

The lumber business at the time was booming, and Ferry, like many other entrepreneurial men of the day, got involved and made himself a good-sized fortune. When Ferry arrived in Grand Haven, he encountered huge two- to three-hundred-year-old pines, filled with countless stories of the ages but also filled with money for the lumber barons. When Ferry passed away on December 30, 1867, at the age of seventy-one, he had $120,000, roughly $1.7 million by today's standards.

The Ferry family wasn't your typical family by any means. Success seemed to run in their blood. Noah Ferry, William's fourth son, taught in Chicago for a few years, started a logging business and set up the town of Montague, naming it after his father, in Muskegon County. When the Civil War broke out, Noah felt honor bound to join in the effort and, in 1862, organized a group of men called the White River Guard to fight in the war. Sadly, Noah was shot in the head and killed during the Battle of Gettysburg on July 2, 1863, at the age of thirty-two. He was given the highest military honors after his death, and his body was returned to and laid to rest in Grand Haven. His body was the first to be interred in Lake Forest Cemetery, long before the property was even deeded as a cemetery. The Ferrys had wanted a special burial place for their son away from the general population.

Thomas White Ferry, the third son in the family, was extremely successful in government, holding positions beginning with county clerk at age twenty-one all the way up to the U.S. Senate. In 1883, Thomas became the president of the Mackinaw Parks Commission and was instrumental in helping make Mackinaw Island the preserve and tourist destination it is today. Thomas was also one of the few selected people to escort President Lincoln's body back to his hometown of Springfield, Illinois, after his assassination. With such family history, it is no wonder that the family still hangs around their human remains.

The Ferry tombstones are beautiful, and it is easy to see how stories spill out of young mouths while visiting Ferry Hill in the middle of a dark night. Amanda Ferry's tomb is ornately carved and remarkably intact for its age. William Ferry's grave is one of the more eerie tombs in the cemetery, with its inscription: First Toil—Then Rest, First Grace—Then Glory. The current legend says that William Ferry is angry that his tomb has been disturbed. He now watches over the cemetery as a silent, glowing reminder to any trespassers to stay away from what remains of his and his family's gravestones. Many people like to say that the tree next to the Ferry tomb has something to do with the haunting. Sure, it looks creepy, having been carved up with symbols over the years, but that is just the byproduct of people wanting to leave their marks behind.

It's not only the top of Ferry Hill that's haunted; there's also something freaky about the stairs leading up to the burial grounds!

THE STAIRWAY TO HELL

Ferry Hill is reached by taking a moderately hefty trek up uneven wooden steps. Stories say that the staircase guiding you up to the Ferrys will show you your death when you reach the top. According to the legend, when a person has been buried in Lake Forest, his soul goes to the bottom of the steps and walks up. If he is greeted by a white light, he is going to heaven. But if a white light doesn't show up, he turns around and begrudgingly walks back down the stairs, awaiting his trip to hell.

Nearly every cemetery with an old staircase in it has a legend attached to it. Just to illustrate legends surrounding staircases in cemeteries, Carpenter's Cemetery in Brazil, Indiana, has a similar set of stairs leading up to a burial ground. The legend is so popular that many locals have renamed the place Hundred Steps Cemetery. The Indiana legend says that at midnight, you must count the stairs as you go up. When you get to the top, turn around and look out into the open area in front of you. The cemetery's first caretaker will appear to you in a vision and show you how you will die. On your way down, count the steps again, and if you come up with a different number than you did coming up, you will die the way the caretaker showed you.

Care to take a visit to Hundred Steps Cemetery and count your steps? Many have, and so far, no one has seen their "vision of death." This is just one story to illustrate the many legends that surround stairways in cemeteries. It's only natural that little Grand Haven has its very own "portal to hell" in its staircase.

AUTHOR'S PERSONAL STORY

Investigations conducted by Michigan's Otherside and others haven't revealed much in the way of genuine paranormal activity. As a rule, most cemeteries aren't haunted, but they are the first place anyone thinks of when trying to find a ghost. Since the cemetery is located in one of our hometowns, we figured it would be worth checking it out a couple of times. Starting with the show *Ghost Hunters* on the Sci Fi (now Syfy) channel, and many other subsequent copycat shows, paranormal awareness has skyrocketed. Kids and thrill seekers have all taken trips to the cemetery in

Haunted Lake Forest Cemetery

The Stairway to Hell of Lake Forest Cemetery. *Photo by Amberrose Hammond.*

the hopes of seeing the elusive "Blue Man," but so far, only imagination seems to accompany everyone on their way out rather than a blue spirit.

As for anything scary or menacing, we have found nothing—no strange pictures, no concrete electronic voice phenomena. Most of the psychics we have worked with have received feelings of sadness while visiting the place. But it's not Ferry Hill where we had interesting experiences; the cemetery's Potter's Field held the strangest moments for us.

During one of our first investigations at the cemetery, we brought a psychic who had no knowledge of the place. I was guiding him around the cemetery when he suddenly stopped in front of the Potter's Field. He started to get extreme amounts of sadness and felt that something was trying to follow him from the area. He looked above him, and the only way he could describe what he saw in his mind was "dark oil slicks darting around in the air." He felt whatever was there was troubled and very unhappy. As we started to walk away, he felt something following him. He turned around and, in a firm voice, told whatever it was, "You are to stay here. You cannot follow me any longer." We continued on.

I later explained to him that the area he had had such trouble with was the cemetery's Potter's Field, an area where unknowns, bodies washed up by Lake Michigan, poor folks, people without family and many other unfortunate souls were all buried, with the large majority of the graves unmarked. For such a small area, local researchers have speculated that there are over one thousand bodies buried in the plot. The name Potter's Field is a biblical reference to Matthew 27:3-8 in the New Testament. The first body to ever be buried in the Potter's Field was a victim of the ill-fated ship *Ironsides*. It is also one of the oldest tombstones in the cemetery.

Maybe the Blue Man apparition is nothing more than the byproduct of an over-excited imagination, but either way, stories will always haunt the cemetery. In the minds of believers, the Blue Man will continue to sit perched on his hill, along with all of the other departed souls of Lake Forest Cemetery, waiting and watching for all eternity to make sure that his town continues to prosper as he intended.

While walking in Lake Forest one day, stop at the Stairway to Hell, climb up the winding wooden steps, look around at the tombstones of the people who started a town—early pioneers, a fallen soldier of Gettysburg—and take a moment for these early settlers. Maybe, just maybe, you'll have a visit from William M. Ferry, or the Blue Man, as he's known in the afterlife.

HAUNTED NUNICA CEMETERY

Established in 1883, Nunica Cemetery, in the tiny town of Nunica, has gained the reputation of being one of the most haunted cemeteries along Michigan's west coast. A rather small, unassuming sort of place becomes a whole different story when the sun sets, or so the stories say. A dirt driveway winding through the cemetery leads you past tombstones and huge trees with crooked branches shading the graves beneath them. Nunica is unique in that it allowed, for a time, families to make homemade graves and tombstones for their loved ones. Homemade crosses adorned with pictures and trinkets that meant something to the deceased used to take up a lot of the back end of the graveyard. Compared to the more traditional cemeteries in the area, the folk art throughout Nunica gave it a "backwoods," spooky feeling.

So much ghost-hunting traffic has entered Nunica Cemetery in recent years that Crockery Township has set up opening and closing times and will not tolerate people inside the cemetery at night. That means you'll have to pull up a chair by the entrance sign and look through your night-vision scopes in hopes of seeing the nighttime activity of the cemetery's otherworldly residents. Otherwise, the cemetery can be enjoyed during the daytime. Who says that ghosts only come out at night?

Nunica Cemetery was first investigated for paranormal activity by the West Michigan Ghost Hunters Society. In the early days of ghost hunting, before many of the TV shows and all the excitement about ghost hunting, Michigan only had a few paranormal teams. West Michigan

A wooden cross in Nunica Cemetery. *Photo by Amberrose Hammond*

Ghost Hunter's Society got its start in 1999, and Nunica Cemetery was one of its early explorations. Nicole Bray, WMGHS founder, hadn't heard crazy stories or legends about the cemetery. In fact, she had never heard of the cemetery at all! While driving down M 104, she happened to notice an old sign hidden behind some bushes that read "Cemetery." Excited to explore a new place, she returned two weeks later with some basic investigative equipment: a digital thermometer, camera and an EMF (electromagnetic field) detector. Being inside a place that should not be giving off any type of electromagnetic field, her meter was going crazy. Nicole suspected that the area might be paranormally active after she got a few unusual photos.

When Nicole was first investigating the cemetery, many of the pictures taken were of what people refer to as "orbs." After learning that many of the early photos were dust, moisture or, in fact, "digital duds" caused by the new technology of digital cameras still in its infancy at the time, Nicole said of her early pictures:

> *I think about 80 percent of them were probably naturally made by dust, grass molds, etc., but 20 percent were possibly the real thing. One small cemetery with a 20 percent chance of capturing paranormal activity is still a high percentage. I have removed all the old orb photos from Nunica Cemetery on our website and I am still left with what I believe are eighty-five positive photos.*

Nicole did some research on the area and discovered that Nunica had suffered an influenza outbreak in the 1920s, a possible reason for the seemingly high numbers of children buried in the cemetery. While not confirmed, she also heard that the front part of the cemetery, which is lacking burials and tombstones, is an old Indian burial ground. There's a large tree toward the front of the cemetery as well where people seemed to always feel something strange. While taking a tour one day with a Crockery Township worker, Nicole was told that, in the 1930s, a man hanged himself in the tree. There is a branch missing from the tree, and there has been speculation that if the man did in fact hang himself there, the branch was cut down to bring his body to the ground. The truth is probably lost in the past, but Nicole believes that if the hanging did occur, it could explain "why all the paranormal activity around that tree seems to be captured about fifteen to twenty feet in the air."

Nicole feels that Nunica had a different "vibe" to it when she first went inside, compared to other cemeteries in the area. Nicole remembers that during her early days of investigating, the place had a "draining effect" on the investigators and the equipment:

> *The "residents of Nunica" seemed to feed off our energy and energy from our equipment. I know that whenever I went home after being at Nunica Cemetery, I always felt completely drained and slept almost twelve hours the next day. The only other location that has ever affected me that way are the Gettysburg Battlefields.*

The cemetery is also known for another paranormal phenomenon called shadow people. There are many theories regarding what these entities could be. Some feel that they are just another form of spirit activity; others believe that they are more malicious in nature, appearing to people at night while they sleep and causing feelings of panic. Some even feel they could be part of another dimension bleeding through into ours. The theories are endless. Nicole encountered shadow people in the cemetery at first, but since the cemetery changed its policy on "homemade tombstones" and cleaned the place up in recent years—trimming wild bushes and taking down a lot of trees along the sides of the property—Nicole mused:

> It doesn't even feel the same there. It's like a reverse reaction to the theory of "renovation can stir up spirits." Like the removal of all the decorations and cutting down of the trees killed off all the paranormal activity, or maybe "they" were just sick of all the visitors!

With all of the strange photos, equipment failures and the feeling of being drained, Nicole wasn't ready for her most amazing experience in the cemetery to date. WMGHS held public ghost hunts, and it was during the society's second hunt in Nunica that the night ended with a spooky finale.

A group of people who had joined the tour in the hopes of experiencing something paranormal was standing in an area of the cemetery where a high number of children are buried. All of the people suddenly experienced a dramatic cold spot. While the cold wrapped around the group, one of the members heard a little boy's voice, and the cold suddenly went away.

Curious about what was going on with the group of people, Nicole walked up to them with two other investigators, when one of the investigators near her took a sudden inhale of breath. Nicole remembered:

> I didn't have but more than a second to think about what may be going on with her as I was assaulted by this "force." It was the sensation of freezing from the inside-out, like someone forced a bucket of ice down into my stomach and I literally could not breath for a few moments. You

would have a sharp intake of breath and that was all you could do until it passed. A few seconds after my experience, I heard the investigator to the right of me take a harsh inhale. After the incident was over and we all began to talk, all three of us had had the same exact feeling and experience.

Nicole firmly believes that a spirit traveled through them while escaping from the group of people who had first experienced the cold spot. Could it have been the spirit of a little boy? Nicole will always remember that night. "To my dying day," she said, "I am never going to forget what that felt like."

THE PLAYFUL GHOST OF "MR. BOND"

Nunica's most famous spirit would be that of "Mr. Bond," as he has been named. When investigators started to constantly feel things in the vicinity of his tombstone, they wondered if it was the active spirit of this Civil War veteran. Mr. Bond seems to especially like the ladies and has been known to touch their backsides and play with their hair. Was Mr. Bond a charmer in life?

Joel A. Bond was born in New York State in 1846. At some point, his family moved to Michigan's west coast. In 1864, Joel turned eighteen and enlisted in the Twenty-first Michigan Infantry as part of Company G. The Twenty-first was composed of the majority of Michigan's western counties. The war ended one year later, and the infantry was disbanded on June 25, 1865, so Joel's time spent as a soldier in the Civil War was short. He came back home to Nunica, married a woman named Ann and enjoyed the rest of his life as a farmer. He was also an early pioneer in establishing Nunica as a town, having been a supervisor for Crockery Township as well as holding other office positions. Like many men of his day, he was involved with fraternities such as the Odd Fellows and was active in the affairs of Ottawa County.

Joel and his wife lived on a forty-acre farm in Wright Township in the later years of his life. Age was creeping up on him, and his health was failing. The winter months of 1913 were rough on him. When April

Mr. Bond's Civil War tombstone. *Photo by Amberrose Hammond.*

came about and spring started to thaw the frozen Michigan ground, Joel started to feel better. He found himself in good enough health to start plowing his fields again, preparing them for the warmer weather ahead. Joel's friend Frank Skeels came over to help him on Friday, April 18. The two got busy on the field. Frank was guiding the plow and Joel was steering the horses when Joel suddenly collapsed onto the ground. Frank ran to his friend's side, but there was nothing that could be done. Joel's heart had given out on him, and his obituary, published in the *Coopersville Observer* on April 25, 1913, was bluntly titled, "Dropped Dead in his Field."

Not much is known about Joel's personality, besides being a hard worker and always active in community affairs. If it is indeed Joel A. Bond haunting that corner of the cemetery, he must have been a flirty, playful type of guy. His tombstone is a small, Civil War stone engraved with just his name and his company.

TAKE HER COLD HAND

Author's Personal Story

Nunica Cemetery gets extremely dark at night if there's no moonlight. There are a few lights from the nearby highway and gas station off in the distance. One night in the cemetery on an investigation with WMGHS, I had an experience that I still can't explain to this day. I found my left hand and arm getting very, very cold. A few investigators felt that there was the spirit of a little girl who liked to hang onto your hand or cling to your leg as you walked through parts of the cemetery. Another investigator with me pulled out a temperature gauge and took a reading of the ambient air temperature around my hand. The digital readout showed twenty degrees. It was late summer, and the temperature that night was somewhere in the seventies. Half expecting to see a child appear out of nowhere hanging onto my hand, I walked for a bit with my hand outstretched until, eventually, the extreme cold left. It was sad to think that there could have been the lonely little spirit of a child hanging on to a stranger's hand for some form of comfort.

HELPFUL SPIRITS?

Nunica Cemetery is surrounded by woods, and some of the outer edges have uneven ground where the sandy dirt was dug out a bit. Tom Maat of Michigan's Otherside can remember walking around and suddenly feeling a hand on his shoulder from behind. He turned around and found

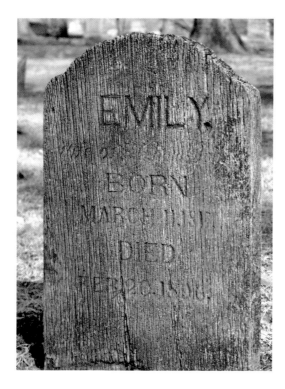

The old, unusual wooden tombstone of Emily in Nunica Cemetery. *Photo by Amberrose Hammond.*

no one there, but when he started to look around, he noticed in front of him a small drop off. It was nothing major, but the stumble would have been enough to cause a few bruises and possibly a sprained ankle.

THE MAINTENANCE SHED AND THE LADY IN WHITE

Cemetery legend says that a maintenance man was on top of the storage shed when he fell off and broke his neck, quickly ending his life. No one knows for sure if this is true or not, but that's been the story going around the campfire for years. Regardless of the validity of the story, many people have reported strange feelings by the shed. Tom remembers one night years ago when he and other ghost hunters heard the sound of a horse and wagon over by the maintenance shed. Of course, nothing was there, but more than one person heard the sound. Was it something residual in the area from days long ago?

Haunted Nunica Cemetery

The hill where the lady in white apparition has been seen in Nunica Cemetery among strange cold spots. *Photo by Amberrose Hammond.*

It can't be a proper haunted cemetery without a "lady in white." Cemeteries all around the United States claim to have one of these apparitions floating around from time to time, scaring the life out of the living as they wander around the tombstones at night. A lady in white has been seen in the part of the cemetery that is on a slight hill. Not much is heard about this apparition, nor have many run into people who have seen it—if, in fact, it is really there at all. But enough stories have circulated to keep the idea of her alive.

Nicole Bray believes that half of the experiences had by people in Nunica are probably brought on by over-active imaginations, but some rare moments are very real, especially for the person to whom they are happening. With the help of Mr. Bond and the rest of the lively spirits in Nunica, the cemetery will continue to scare and delight paranormal enthusiasts for years to come.

THE GHOSTS OF
BOWER'S HARBOR INN

Bower's Harbor Inn rests on Old Mission Peninsula in northern Michigan by Traverse City. The building consists of two restaurants: the Bower's Harbor Inn and the Bowery, located behind the home in what used to be an old barn, the first building on the property. Along with good food and its own winery, Bower's Harbor Inn is also home to a ghostly legend.

THE LEGEND OF GENEVIEVE'S GHOST

Paranormal activity in Bower's Harbor Inn has been reported for years and years. The usual sounds of raps on walls, doors opening and closing, lights going on and off by themselves and objects moving on their own are all commonplace in the Bower's Harbor Inn. For as long as anyone who has known about the ghosts of the home can remember, the common legend told goes something like this:

One of the home's first owners, J.W. Stickney, a lumber baron, and his wife, Genevieve, still haunt their former home. Some have reported coming face to face with the ghostly body of J.W. Stickney in the home's elevator. Others have reported seeing Genevieve in a mirror that belonged to her. The legend says that Genevieve was a larger woman, and the mirror was specially designed to make her appear slimmer when she looked at her reflection. The Bower's Harbor website states:

The Ghosts of Bower's Harbor Inn

In 1964, a patron rushed downstairs shaken, her face ashen. She had been standing before Genevieve's gilt-edged mirror. "I was alone in the hallway and noticed another woman looking in the mirror behind me." Her hair was pulled back in a bun, just as Genevieve had worn hers.

Genevieve continued to gain weight, and eventually her husband had to install an elevator for her to get to each floor of the house. According to the Bower's Inn website, Genevieve hanged herself in the elevator shaft. Her husband had been having an affair with Genevieve's nurse, and when he died, he left his money to the nurse and only the house to Genevieve. This sank her into a severe depression and resulted in her suicide, thus the reason that her ghost still resides at the home.

Everyone from the staff to the diners have experienced paranormal moments at the main restaurant and also in the second restaurant at the back of the house, the Bowery, which is the oldest part of the property. Eerie encounters include everything from faucets turning on and off on their own, mysterious lights appearing out of nowhere and even sightings of Genevieve herself. One of the most paranormally active places in the building is Genevieve's sitting room. For the most part, many of the strange things that have happened there throughout the years to guests and workers can be blamed on imagination and an old house with drafts and creaks and all sorts of "house arthritis."

Every legend has an origin, and how the Bower's Harbor Inn story got started is just as much of a mystery as the ghosts who live there. In reality, the current legend doesn't match up with the true history behind the people's spirits that are said to haunt the home. Genevieve was born in 1863 and was described as being a small person, hardly like the image the legend portrays. She married Charles Stickney, and after discovering an old farmhouse and land for sale on Old Mission Peninsula about 1909, they fixed up the old farmhouse and called it home in the summer months. The two loved the beautiful surroundings and were devastated when a fire broke out in the house sometime in the 1920s. But out of that fire came the beautiful home that still stands today. With extensive attention to detail and expensive embellishments throughout, the Stickneys had their very own palace to call home.

Charles and Genevieve had quite the life together and seemed ideal soul mates. Genevieve developed heart disease and passed away on March 15, 1947. She actually died in Grand Rapids, Michigan, at the Pantlind Hotel, which is now the Amway Grand Plaza Hotel in downtown Grand Rapids, also rumored to be haunted. The Stickneys lived there during the winter months.

It is wonderful when someone finally comes along and questions these old stories. What is the truth behind them? Is there any at all? Authors Kathleen Tedsen and Beverlee Rydel, for their book *Haunted Travels of Michigan*, discovered the truth about Bower's Harbor Inn while researching the legend. They discovered that Mr. Stickney did in fact leave his entire estate to Genevieve's nurse, Kathryn. It was also discovered, after speaking to Kathryn's daughter, that Genevieve and Charles both had failing health, and the nurse caught Genevieve one day "tampering" with Charles's medication. Was she trying to end his life first? The truth will probably never come out. Was a relationship or bond forming between the nurse and Charles? It would seem so.

When Genevieve passed on, her body had swelled to large proportions, possibly lending to the stories of her being a "big lady." After her death, Charles didn't like the idea of being alone and moved in with the widowed nurse and her children. It is easy to make assumptions about what was going through Genevieve's mind during the last days of her life. Was she angry that the nurse was going to inherit everything that she and her husband had owned? Was her illness causing dementia to set in?

An interview with author Kathleen Tedsen about Bower's Harbor Inn gives a little more insight into the spirits of the home. Kathleen said:

This is a story particularly close to our hearts. We put so much time into the research (months and months) and with the help of this amazing historian, eventually we were able to discover the truth. Initially we were disappointed to discover the Legend of Genevieve was false. It is, after all, such a great ghost story. In the end, however, we were very happy and very excited to get the true story out. We found that the truth is more fascinating, more intriguing, than the legend and brings with it an even more mysterious edge: who actually haunts Bower's Harbor Inn?

While conducting an investigation at Bower's Inn for their book, Kathleen remembered her experience in the elevator that is always said to be haunted. As Kathleen got into the elevator, an indescribable feeling washed over her:

I was surprised and overwhelmed at the same time, and I am certainly not a sensitive. Truth is, I don't have a sensitive bone in my body! So, when I walked into the elevator and closed the door, what happened was completely unexpected. It was an intense feeling of sadness, hopelessness and loss. It was the first time something like this had happened to me. Time, literally, slipped away. I became lost in these intense feelings. If my coauthor Bev hadn't come to tell me it was time to leave, I truly don't know how long I would have stayed in there.

Several months after that elevator moment, Kathleen would speak about the events and the same feelings of sadness would return:

Beverly and I do believe there is some type of paranormal activity going on at Bower's Harbor Inn. This is based on the EVPs (electronic voice phenomena) we collected (which are thought to be the voices of the dead), the light in an upstairs room turning on and off when Bev and I left the restaurant that we got on video and a compelling video recorded in the back restaurant. We still believe additional investigations are needed and evidence collected before it can officially be called "haunted."

Regardless of the history of the old house, there have been far too many paranormal occurrences to claim that nothing is there. Whether it's the Stickneys, just Genevieve or the original builders of the old farmhouse from whom the Stickneys bought the property, there are spirits staying around that don't have any plans of moving on. Anyone visiting Old Mission Peninsula will have to make a dinner stop at Bower's and see if they are paid a visit by the resident ghosts.

THE GHOST LOVERS
OF CASTLE PARK

It is hard to resist a good ghost story that involves two doomed lovers, especially on sparkling Lake Macatawa, with its beautiful mansions, summer homes and old Castle Park, that closed to the public in 1985 but was once a popular summer resort.

Escaping life in the Prussian Empire, Michael Schwarz, a retired real-estate promoter, came with his family to Holland along Lake Michigan's shore to start a new life. He wanted his family to be far removed from the rest of the world, and in 1890, he constructed a huge, three-story, castle-like structure. There would be no need to visit bustling cities. Everything they needed would be at "the Castle," as it became known. Schwarz realized that his idea of a feudal-style castle, completely disengaged from society, wasn't going to work out as well as he hoped. Six daughters and two sons who were used to city life no doubt made life miserable; perhaps this was one of the reasons Schwarz abandoned his plans of living a secluded life and moved his family into the city of Holland in 1892. The Castle was put up for sale only two years after it was built.

In 1893, Reverend John H. Parr discovered the three-story castle while visiting the area. He was headmaster at the Chicago Preparatory School. Realizing that the building was perfect, he bought it instantly and created a summer camp for kids. There was something about the land on which Castle Park sat; when parents came to visit their kids at summer camp, they found that along with their kids, they didn't want to go back home either. Feeling that there was something special about the place, the reverend and his wife closed their prep school in 1896 and spent the rest of their time turning the castle house into an inn and developing the area as a resort. The idea of the "resort" was a new and popular idea sweeping across the United States, and Lake Michigan's beautiful beaches and shorelines provided the perfect place for Americans to spend their newfound leisure time. The parents of the summer camp kids were the first to buy lots, and many people followed suit. If someone didn't own property within the resort, they could rent a room at the inn inside the castle.

Reverend Parr's nephew, Carter Pannell Brown, had the most influence on the park's early days. Carter was just a baby when he first visited Castle Park, coming over on a rocky boat ride across Lake Michigan from Chicago and later working for his uncle as the transporter for guests coming to Castle Park by boat. Carter took over ownership of the resort park in 1917. Many years later, when Castle Park became an association, residents in 1985 eventually bought out the castle structure, and its days as a public inn ended. The castle was restored to its former beauty and Victorian splendor and is now used as a private building for the association members.

It has been said that the castle was an inspiration for L. Frank Baum's castle in the *Wizard of Oz*. Frank Baum spent many summers in Holland, writing one of the world's most beloved children's novels of all time.

Legends about ghosts and spirits surrounding the structure have always wandered the Holland area. A German-inspired castle, once in the middle of nowhere, was bound to create a story or two. When Castle Park was open as a resort, it published a small article on its "resident ghost." The legend involves one of Michael Schwarz's daughters running away with a lover. Two endings exist of this lakeshore legend.

The most popular ending of the story tells of the daughter running off into the night to elope with her lover, a Dutch boy from Holland, Michigan. Schwarz heard word of the couple's plans to wed and went off in search of the secret wedding. He arrived just in time to stop the couple from exchanging vows. Schwarz pulled his daughter away from her lover and locked her up in the castle until she agreed to never see her lover again. The simpler ending states that Schwarz tried to track them down on horseback to stop the marriage but failed to arrive in time, witnessing his daughter and unfortunate son-in-law kiss for the first time as man and wife. Castle Park residents told how her ghost could "be seen in the tower on moonlit nights, looking toward Holland and her lost love."

While Schwarz's daughter went on to lead a normal life, getting married and having children, it seems that her true love was never fulfilled in life, so she continues to look for her Dutch boy in death, hoping that their souls will meet up at some point. Today, Castle Park is listed on the Historic Register, but it is not open to the public. It can still be enjoyed from the road, however, and maybe while driving past it in the night, you'll see the daughter looking out the tower window for her long lost Dutch boy.

GRAND TRAVERSE LIGHTHOUSE

When the tourists have gone away for the day and there's no one left inside the light, a spirit or two might still linger in the Grand Traverse Lighthouse. Built in 1858, the light is located at the tip of the Leelanau Peninsula and is part of the Leelanau State Park. Also known as the Northport Light, its red roof and white painted brick make it a charming building, one hardly suited to ghosts, but it appears that the light is still the home of one of its former (dead) lightkeepers.

After Grand Traverse was automated in 1972 with a boring, skeletal steel tower nearby, the old lighthouse building and the once beautiful light were left to fend for themselves. The buildings became run-down and went uncared for until locals, not wanting the light to crumble, formed the Grand Traverse Lighthouse Foundation in 1985 and opened the light to the public as a museum in 1986. Over $1.5 million has been raised since 1985 to save the light, and it is a constant work in progress to keep it restored.

A lighthouse wouldn't be complete without a resident ghost within its walls. It seems that every lighthouse is haunted by its former keeper, forever walking up and down the spiral, black iron staircase of the tower. Stairways are another matter when it comes to haunted lighthouses. When we travel upstairs, we exert far more energy than when walking on level ground, and lighthouse stairs are usually no picnic to walk up. Imagine year after year, day after day, walking up those stairs to tend to the lens. One of the most common paranormal occurrences in lighthouses is the sound of phantom footsteps going up and down

The Grand Traverse Lighthouse. *Photo by www. istockphoto.com/sparkia.*

the stairs. It is sometimes believed that the footsteps heard so often on lighthouse steps are just the residual energy leftover from years of keepers traveling up them.

Lighthouses along Michigan's west coast are part of our nautical heritage and should be preserved at all costs. Many lighthouses are remote or are not open to the public; many are now museums, open to the public for visits in the summer months. The staff might not always be thrilled when visitors ask about the ghosts rather than the history, but the ghosts bring many curiosity seekers to these places, and the history unfolds for them as they learn the story behind the resident spirits.

Stef Staly is the executive director of the lighthouse museum. Having gone to school for museum administration, this is the perfect job for her, and she has been at the light for over ten years. When asked about the ghost of the light, she states, in a no-nonsense tone, that she personally hasn't experienced anything of the ghostly sort, but others at the light have encountered footsteps, phantom sounds and moments of strangeness that couldn't be explained.

People have reported hearing someone with hard-soled shoes walking on the wooden floors. Voices have been heard in the bathroom when no one else is around and in the hall going to the tower. People have felt someone brush past them and have seen images of a man taking his shoes off, perhaps after a hard day's work at the light. According to one psychic, the ghost haunting the light is, in fact, former lightkeeper Captain Peter Nelson.

Captain Nelson was a ship captain. He was keeper of the light from October 1874 to July 11, 1890. Born in Copenhagen, Denmark, Peter Nelson was a determined man. From a young age, he was a cabin boy on a ship, and as he grew up, he took a chance by jumping off the boat he worked on as it left a New York harbor and swam to shore. He became captain of his own ship, the *Venus*, on the Great Lakes when he was in his thirties. Sailing into the area that would one day become Traverse City, the captain purchased land and settled down in 1855. He got married and had his first child at the age of fifty-nine. In an online article written by his great-great-great-granddaughter on Mynorth.com, she recalled that he was the only one of seven brothers who did not die at sea. He is buried on land, and maybe that causes his soul to be restless. Nelson passed away in February 1892.

A few deaths circumvent the lighthouse that could also add to the ghostly occurrences at the light. They could be the ghosts of lightkeeper John Marken and his wife, Bernice, both of whom died on Christmas Eve 1967 in a car accident. Or it could be the ghost of a Coast Guard man who died of a heart attack at the lighthouse, or a woman who died in the kitchen of unknown causes. The only lightkeeper to actually die at the light was Dr. Henry Schetterly, who was keeper from 1862 to 1873.

The museum doesn't play up the ghost aspect of the lighthouse. The ghosts aren't the stars of the show, but regardless of who is haunting the place, employees, volunteers and visitors over the years have experienced one thing or another that couldn't be explained and left them wondering who still watches over the place in the afterlife.

THE LEGEND OF DOGMAN

*If you decide to tell the tale of the legend of the Michigan Dogman, be sure to install
a hint of doubt into your voice, for at the end of the night if the children believe, the
Dogman they may receive!*
—*Michigan author Chad Stuemke*

T he year was 1987, and radio deejay Steve Cook from Traverse City
started a frenzy when he played a song on April Fool's day simply
called "The Legend." The song's lyrics were about a mysterious creature
that has become known as Dogman—a half man, half dog creature
standing over seven feet tall that prowls the woods of Michigan. Cook
had always been interested in folklore, ghosts and mysterious creatures,
and this interest inspired his lyrics. The lyrics used local places in northern
Michigan, such as Bower's Harbor, as settings. The song told a gruesome
tale of animals dying of fright and a priest finding sinister claw marks
slashed into the church door. By all means, it seemed a harmless prank,
until people started to call into the radio station claiming that they had
seen the creature described in the song! That same year, reports about a
cabin being attacked by a dog filled local papers and found their way into
USA Today. Dogman has been popular ever since.

One of the foremost researchers on the Dogman phenomena is Linda
Godfrey. Linda started to study Dogman after hearing reports about
the beast in Wisconsin but soon found out that many of the Dogman
sightings were also being reported in northwest Michigan. She noticed
that many sightings of this creature seemed to center on Native American

An artist's rendition of Dogman. *Original art by Steven Mayes.*

burial and effigy mounds. Effigy mounds were typically in the shape of an animal. Traverse City had a large amount of mounds, and ironically, there have been many Dogman sightings in that area of the west coast.

Chad Stuemke, a Michigan author and avid researcher of all things strange and mysterious, lives in northwest Michigan. Chad is no stranger to the Dogman story and feels that some of the Dogman legend and inspiration goes back to Native American tales of "shape shifters." Native Americans believe that one can change his "mental shape" to take on aspects and traits of a totem animal. The totem animal is something that is always with you and protects you on your life journey. But some stories tell of Native Americans actually physically turning into their totem. Chad states:

> *The explanations for the belief and possible existence of Dogman are endless. Scientifically speaking, belief in and of itself may be a large part of the equation. This leads to the question: Could the belief of*

ancient Native Americans in conjunction with our own personal beliefs be adequate to bring this creature into fruition? As the legend of the Michigan Dogman continues to grow, so has the number of eyewitness accounts. This seems normal considering the more that become aware of the legend, the more who will "think" they have seen the creature. This admittedly is the most likely scenario. But there is always that slight possibility that it is the other way around, and that it is the belief in and of itself that is allowing this creature to literally step into our perceived reality.

Ever since 1987 and Steve Cook's song, people truly believe that there is more to the tale than just an April Fool's joke. At the time of the song's release, people took it very seriously. Tom Maat remembers hearing the song while living on the east side of Michigan. He asked his friends if they wanted to go camping up near Traverse City, and none of his friends would go. They had all heard about Dogman and were scared about encountering it. More than twenty years after the songs first release, "The Legend" has become a tradition in northwest Michigan. Whether the song was a premonition or a novelty, it certainly awoke a creature that won't fade out of Michiganders' minds anytime soon.

THE OLD TRAVERSE CITY STATE HOSPITAL

It should never be forgotten, that every object of interest that is placed in or about a hospital for the insane, that even every tree that buds, or every flower that blooms, may contribute in its small measure to excite a new train of thought, and perhaps be the first step towards bringing back to reason, the morbid wanderings of a disordered mind.

—Thomas Story Kirkbride

A book looking at haunted and spooky places along Michigan's west coast can't go without mentioning the Traverse City State Hospital. Mental asylums have always been considered the holy grail of paranormal activity and creepiness combined. Tales of lobotomies, patients strapped into straightjackets and other cruel stories of how the insane were treated circulate around these old buildings like vultures. Many of the old asylums from the nineteenth century have been torn down, but a few still stand. First known as the Northern Michigan Asylum for the Insane, this hospital opened its doors in 1885 during a time when mental health was being looked at through a different perspective.

THE ASYLUM BUILDING AS HEALER

During the mid-1800s, mental health was being looked at as a real issue that could be dealt with through proper means. It wasn't being ignored anymore. In the past, the "insane" were locked up and forgotten about

A turret of the Traverse City State Hospital before renovations. *Photo by Amberrose Hammond.*

or treated similar to wild animals. "Insanity" was considered to be the "devil" lurking within a person rather than a valid health condition. The possibility that people could be cured of their mental ailments was a welcome concept as the world entered an industrial revolution and the pace of life started to speed up.

To escape the everyday trials of life that some doctors felt brought on mental illness, a movement called Moral Treatment and the idea of the "therapeutic landscape" were formed. These were concepts that looked at a person's environment and how it influenced them. If someone struggling with mental problems could retreat to a peaceful area, with light work to keep busy and beautiful surroundings, it was believed that many of their ailments would slip away.

Mental hospitals in the nineteenth century grew quickly in the United States, with three built in Michigan between 1858 and 1885. They were in Kalamazoo, Pontiac and Traverse City. The design of the hospital was thought to influence the patient's mental state—one of the philosophies behind the therapeutic landscape belief.

THE KIRKBRIDE PHILOSOPHY

The Traverse City State Hospital, along with the Kalamazoo and Pontiac asylums, was modeled after the Kirkbride plan for mental hospitals. Thomas Story Kirkbride was one of the original founders of the American Psychiatric Association and set the standard for what he believed was good hospital architecture and design. Most of the hospitals built in the United States during the 1800s followed what became known as the Kirkbride plan, first published in 1854. Similar to the idea of feng shui, Kirkbride believed that buildings could hold a certain "curative power." Gardens, exotic trees and greenhouses for yearlong flowers were all part of Kirkbride's "therapeutic landscape." It was believed that just being within the asylum building could have a restorative effect on a patient. Many contemporaries of Kirkbride felt that this was all a waste of time and failed to look at the real problems inflicting many asylum patients. Picking out what colors and curtains would look best was considered neglectful. Perhaps it wasn't the perfect cure, but it was a step forward in the humane treatment of the mentally ill.

Kirkbride believed in the power of huge buildings, and the massive structures left behind during this era of asylum building were impressive and beautiful on a very grand scale. So grand was the scale that many of the buildings couldn't even be torn down, as it would be too costly. The

Traverse City State Hospital was one of these massive buildings, and it sat abandoned for some time after it closed in 1989.

The 1980s brought about healthcare reform for mental health, and money for the institutions went out the door along with the patients. Psychiatric drugs were helping many more people suffering from depression and other forms of mental illness, making the hospitals more and more obsolete, and the huge buildings were becoming too costly to keep open. Many of the mentally ill patients were left to fend for themselves after the doors were closed. Some tried to fit into society the best they could, some became homeless and others continued to seek help elsewhere. Reckless people broke into the hospital to party or vandalize old equipment and walls. Homeless people crawled inside to escape the weather.

ASYLUM GHOSTS

Residents of Traverse City have heard ghostly tales about the hospital for decades. As the buildings began to decay and fall into ruin, the stories about ghosts started to settle within the cracks. The buildings and cottages on the property used to look like the perfect setting for a horror movie. Stories were whispered about lonely ghosts wandering the abandoned halls and the phantom sounds of screaming patients in the night. The place is literally a paranormal investigator's dream, but a formal investigation of the buildings was never conducted due to the danger it imposed. Health hazards—like the mint green lead paint that was peeling from the walls in sheets, the rotting floors and the asbestos—were all factors that kept people out. But that didn't stop people from walking around the grounds (and sometimes still sneaking inside a broken window). People sensitive to spirits who have walked around the buildings have reported an air of depression and sadness. One psychic, with whom I used to work, felt that she had connected with a former nurse who didn't want to leave her "patients behind."

Reports say that ghostly faces peer through the glass windows at night. Radios become nothing but static when driving past buildings. Screams and moans from one of the patient workshop buildings have been reported, and batteries in electronics die quickly, a phenomenon that people feel is the product of a spirit being in the area, draining energy to materialize. At night, a major wave of sadness seems to descend on the buildings, and there are reports of shadowy figures crossing the road in front of cars as they slowly drove past the once decaying buildings. People have also seen lights on in rooms where there wasn't any electricity.

The hospital has certainly seen its share of death through the years. Besides treating mental health, the hospital was also used during tuberculosis epidemics and other illnesses, such as typhoid and influenza. Underground tunnels that connect a few buildings were used by homeless people. But does the hospital have ghostly patients now? Or are the sightings based more on lively imaginations and late-night jaunts past the creepy buildings? Some feel that the woods behind the hospital are infested with evil spirits. Internet rumors on message boards say that rosaries break and bottles of holy water explode if brought near the place.

THE HIPPIE TREE AND MURDER

The hippie tree is a sprawling, old black willow in the woods behind the hospital. The tree has been struck by lightning and is split in two. Growing on its side, it looks as if it is trying to crawl away from something. Smaller willows have continued to grow out of its huge branches, making for a very unusual and eerie site. It has been a location for teen hangouts and random dares in the night for a long time. It seems that the tree got its moniker due to the "hippie-like" and illegal activities that have gone on there over the years.

Some Traverse City people have heard of this legend and some haven't. It is popular with teenagers and young adults and might just be a product of the newest folk story form: Internet urban legend. According to Internet accounts, the legend of the hippie tree says that there were two little boys who were patients at the hospital. The boys went out to play and ventured into some of the underground tunnels that run beneath the buildings. As the boys continued down into the tunnels looking for adventure, they encountered a patient of the hospital who had gone missing and had been living in the tunnels. Terrified, the two boys turned around and started to run fast. After running for some time, one of the boys turned around to find that he was alone. His friend was missing. The boy ran back to the hospital and reported what had happened. The hospital staff searched the tunnels for the missing boy but could only find his St. Raphael necklace and nothing more. A month and a half later, a few of the boy's remains showed up at what is now known as the hippie tree. Whether this legend is purely Internet urban legend or some type of half-truth long forgotten is open to debate.

A SPIRIT IS SET FREE

Take a hike in the woods behind the hospital and you'll find the old water tank, now covered in massive amounts of impressive graffiti. Tom Maat of Michigan's Otherside dreamt about the area before even seeing it. Being sensitive to the other side his whole life, a shudder came through him when he walked up a wooded trail behind one of the hospital buildings and saw the brightly painted water tank.

A few weeks prior to visiting Traverse City with the goal of walking around the grounds of the hospital, Tom had had a strange dream about a person trapped inside of a large water tank. As he explored the tank at Traverse City, he had an urge to climb on top of it. Finding a tree near the tank that looked as if it had been used as a ladder, Tom hoisted himself up and was startled when he found two kids sitting on top, hanging out. He began a conversation with them. They pointed out the ladder going down into the tank. Tom looked down into the murky bottom. Old shoes, garbage and other kinds of refuse lined the floor of the tank. But something kept tugging at him to go inside.

Tom climbed down the ladder into the dark water tank. Not wanting to touch the disgusting, stagnant shallow pool of water below, Tom held on to the ladder with one hand and moved his video camera around the place with his free hand. "Is anyone down here with me today?" Tom asked. As if someone had been waiting for him to ask that, something banged on the inside wall of the tank. The kids and I were sitting on top of the tank, not moving around, and no one was on the ground playing a practical joke.

Tom practices Ama Deus healing, a form of energy work that can help sprits move on. After doing what he was taught to do, Tom feels that whatever was trapped inside the tank was set free that day.

THE HOSPITAL TODAY

The hospital seemed like a lost cause until a developer decided to tackle the massive buildings. In 2000, the Minervini Group from Detroit decided to embark on one of the biggest and perhaps riskiest projects it had ever undertaken: turning the old hospital into a mini metropolis of condos, shopping and other services. But who would want to live in an old asylum? Well how about living or owning a business in a Michigan Tax Free Renaissance Zone, which is what the place is zoned as. Success has been great, and while a few people might shy away from a home that was once an asylum, many have moved in to bring the beauty and life back to the buildings that were originally designed to create a tranquil setting for the mentally disturbed people who lived there.

But those pesky little rumors will always persist about ghosts in the hospital hallways. There are no "gateways to hell" or "evil spirits" waiting around every corner of the place, but there are the very sad memories of the many people who lived and died there. More people left the hospital treated, but some never made it out. Perhaps the ghosts are the spirits of those who died there, not knowing where else to go; or maybe the old place is truly their "therapeutic landscape" as Kirkbride intended.

THE GHOST OF
CHARLES HACKLEY

To a certain extent, I agree with Mr. Carnegie…that it is a crime to die rich.
—Charles Hackley

The above quote explains Charles Henry Hackley's philanthropic attitude perfectly. You can't take your money with you, so why not use it to make your community better! That was Charles Hackley's mentality when it came to the city of Muskegon, a city that he loved dearly and still loves, as he has been spotted all over the place even though he's been dead for over one hundred years.

An inspiration in the city of Muskegon to this day, Charles Henry Hackley was a unique character and left his stamp on a place once known as the Sawdust City. Hackley was born on January 3, 1837, in Michigan City, Indiana. He was blessed with a hardworking spirit and a good mind for making money. In the late 1800s, Muskegon was one of the nation's leading producers of lumber, a large percentage of which helped rebuild Chicago after the Great Fire.

Charles came to Muskegon in 1857 with only seven dollars in his pocket. He worked under his father for a time and continued to move up quickly in his young life, eventually forming a friendship with Thomas Hume and creating Hackley & Hume, one of the largest lumber companies in Michigan, if not the United States. In 1864, he married Julia Ester Moore. They adopted one son, Charles, and raised a foster daughter, Erie Caughell. Hackley amassed a fortune of $18 million, nearly half a billion in today's world.

The Ghost of Charles Hackley

At one point, Muskegon had over thirty millionaires living in the downtown area, but when the lumber industry began to die out, many of the lumber barons packed up and left Muskegon behind. Hackley didn't want to see Muskegon fall by the wayside. In an effort to help the declining economy of Muskegon in the 1890s, Hackley donated a number of buildings, institutions and cash to help the citizens of Muskegon and to create a sense of pride for the people. Hackley admired the words of fellow philanthropist Andrew Carnegie. He read Carnegie's "The Gospel of Wealth" and firmly believed in the message Andrew was giving: spend the money you earned so it is used the way you want before you die.

Hackley followed Carnegie's ideas almost to the letter. Rather than hoard all of the money he had made, he decided to give one-third of it back to the city by creating buildings people could use. The first was the library, followed by a hospital, a park, the Hackley Manual Training School, an art gallery and others.

On May 25, 1888, Charles Henry Hackley made his first big donation to the city by gifting $100,000 for a library and reading room under

The exterior of the Hackley Public Library. *Photo by Tom Maat.*

the stipulation that it always be free and for the public. Half of the money was for the building itself and the other $50,000 was for the purchase of new books. (In 1888, the amount of $100,000 was close to $2 million in today's terms.) The new library was opened and dedicated on October 15, 1890. The entire day was a party, with speeches, music and festivities.

Hackley Public Library looks like something from a fairy tale. The attention to detail and craftsmanship on the outside, as well as the inside, is stunning. Marty Ferriby is the library's tenth director and has worked there since 1994. She was courteous enough to give me a tour of the amazing building. We covered the whole gamut of Hackley history as we traveled through the rooms. The amazing structure is built from pink syenite granite and sandstone, and the style is called Richardsonian Romanesque, which is a combination of Italian, French and Spanish architecture inspired by the eleventh and twelfth centuries. Towers and arches are a popular characteristic of the style, and Hackley Library has plenty of both. The style uses two kinds of stone, two colors of stone, rough stone and asymmetrical designs.

Just being inside the building is enough to inspire a great, gothic ghost story, so it is no surprise that people say the place is haunted. It has everything that goes into a cliché "haunted" place. Gothic-like architecture, old books, stained glass, oil paintings that feel as if they are staring at you and original furniture that creaks with age as you sit down.

One of the outstanding features in the library is a massive set of stained-glass windows that were recently restored. There is a replica of the Book of Kells, a Celtic, illuminated text of the four gospels of the New Testament. They turn a new page once a week. Marty explains that they got it from a company in Europe that makes high-quality reproductions from the real book. As Marty puts it, "it's a very fancy photocopy" but a beautiful addition to the library nevertheless.

As we walk through the library, it's easy to tell just by listening to Marty's words that she cares deeply for the library and its history, along with what Charles Hackley did for the city so long ago. We walk past a bust of Charles near the front entrance, and Marty notes that they dress Charles up for the seasons. He wears a Santa hat at Christmas, a mask at Halloween and has even worn a cape. Marty laughs, "And he wears a size medium T-shirt because of his stone beard." She goes on to say, "People in Muskegon really know who Charles Hackley was and what he contributed to the city. He's an inspiration for us all. He really is." Marty also admits to rubbing the bust's head for good luck when they need it.

But are the stories true? Do ghosts really float between the stacks at Hackley Public Library? Does Charles still enjoy a good book in the midnight hours? When asked about the rumors of Charles Hackley's ghost, Marty is hesitant and chooses her words carefully. "My job is to bring people into the library, not scare them away," she says. The library doesn't ever advertise or play on the rumor of ghosts, even at Halloween.

Some people in the past have noticed the tiny carved faces in the woodwork of Charles Hackley's Victorian house and on the front doors of the library, and they exclaim, "Oh, Charles Hackley believed in Satan!" Marty admits that she's a "hard sell" when it comes to that notion. The faces are simply beautiful details from an elegant past. Hackley wasn't a religious man. He didn't belong to a church and didn't have his funeral in one, either. He no doubt subscribed to his own good thoughts and did what he felt was right in his own heart. When it comes to the ghost of Charles in the library, Marty states, "I'm not going to say whatever is or isn't. But I do know that if we feel a presence, it's a beneficent presence. We have had spiritualists come in and say they feel something 'positive' here."

Besides rumors of ghosts at the library, people say that they see the ghost of Charles all over the city from time to time. Hackley's own home and his good friend Thomas Hume's home are top candidates for spooky stories around town. Hackley began construction on his mansion in 1887 and finished it in 1889. Thomas Hume's home is next door. The homes are magnificent and have been lovingly restored over the years. They are open as museums in the summer months and are well worth the visit.

Carol Williams was living in the old Sibley house near Hackley's mansion in 1989 with two other friends. They were sharing the bathroom and kitchen but all had their own bedrooms. Even though it was twenty years ago, Carol remembers her experience at the house vividly. One night, at about 1:00 a.m., she found herself wide awake

Detail of the front doors of the Hackley Public Library. *Photo by Tom Maat.*

and sitting up in bed. The room was large, and she had a small couch at the foot of her bed. Carol blinked her eyes a couple of times and looked straight ahead at three figures sitting on the couch. Carol remembered, "I looked up and saw this man, woman and toddler. The toddler was sort of climbing on the side of the couch, moving around like any little kid would, but the two adults were stoic and just looking at me." Carol wondered if she was still dreaming but knew that she was wide awake and that her vision was clear.

Within a week's time of having the dream, the friend who owned the house was cleaning the fireplace and, in passing, told Carol, "Hey look what I found!" It was an old photograph. Carol looked closely at the man in the photo and was shocked to see the man who had been sitting on her couch the night she suddenly woke up. Knowing a bit about Charles Hackley, Carol paid a visit to the museum. The photo her roommate had found had been a younger man, not the usual photos of Charles with his long, white, whimsical beard and bald head. She asked the museum worker if they had any pictures of a younger Hackley. The lady showed her a few, confirming that it was, in fact, Charles Hackley in the picture found in the house and it had been Charles at the foot of her bed. Carol told the museum worker what had happened, and the older woman responded, "Oh there's always Charles Hackley sightings in the downtown area. Several people have come into the museum and talked about their sightings."

The Ghost of Charles Hackley

An oil painting of Charles H. Hackley in the Hackley Public Library. *Photo by Tom Maat.*

Charles Hackley passed away on January 10, 1905. He was buried in an elaborate mausoleum with a six-foot granite angel on the top of the tomb at Evergreen Cemetery. His memory is very much alive in the city of Muskegon, and Hackley Day is celebrated every Friday before Memorial Day. The school systems are closed, and the kids get a day off. People forget about their town founders, early pioneers and town history, but not in Muskegon. A poem written on the event of his death said, "Hackley's not dead to me, I see his footprints all over."

So while traveling through Muskegon, visit Hackley's home and make sure to stop by the Hackley Public Library. Pick up a self-guided tour booklet at the reference desk and quietly explore the amazing building. Don't pester the librarians for ghost stories, though. Just go in search of your own and hope that maybe Charles Hackley will poke his bald head around a book stack, extend his arm in a handshake and offer a personal tour from the man himself.

THE FELT MANSION

For many years, this seventeen-thousand-square-foot brick mansion sat abandoned and alone among the tall dune grass and trees by the Saugatuck State Park, until a restoration project began in 2000. Having sat unused for a while, nearly hidden from sight by thick trees and brush, stories about ghosts haunting the home were shared by thrill-seekers and teens. Before the restoration project, its original windows were bricked up, and thick ivy covered large portions of the building.

HISTORY OF THE MANSION

The twenty-five-room mansion was originally completed in 1928 by inventor Dorr E. Felt for his wife, Agnes, and was a summer home for the Chicago family. Agnes sadly died six weeks after the house was completed, in August 1928, and was never able to fully enjoy her beautiful sprawling estate. Dorr Felt, born in 1862, made his millions by creating the comptometer, which was essentially an early version of a calculator. He died a couple years after his wife, in 1930, at the age of sixty-eight.

In 1949, the mansion and property, known as Shore Acres, was sold by the Felt family to the St. Augustine Seminary for boys. The seminary used the carriage house for classrooms and the mansion for housing. Behind the mansion, the seminary built another school. After the school was built, cloistered nuns moved into the mansion in the 1960s. During the 1970s, the State of Michigan began using the property for a state

The front of the historic Felt Mansion. *Photo by Amberrose Hammond.*

police post and tore down the boy's school, putting up in its place the Dunes Correctional Facility, a minimum-security prison.

The Felt Mansion is now on the National Register of Historic Places, as well as the Michigan State Register of Historic Sites, and is a protected site. It has been open and for the public since Laketown Township purchased the property from the state for one dollar. Caring for the area and the mansion helps protect the local dune system surrounding the mansion.

THE GHOST STORIES

The mansion has been a lot of things since its beginning, and it is not surprising to hear about a few ghosts roaming its spacious interior. Soon after the remodeling started, the paranormal activity seemed to start up as well. During the summer of 2001, the West Michigan

Ghost Hunters Society offered ghost tours of the mansion to the public. The tours included the mansion and the nearby run-down Dunes Correctional Facility. All of the money went to help restore the mansion and generated over $3,000. I was lucky enough to attend all of the tours and explore the mansion before most of the restoration began and the ghost tours stopped.

I can say from personal experience that we had some strange stuff happen while on the tours. Doug, of Ghostly Talk Radio, remembers being there and seeing Tom Maat of Michigan's Otherside standing very close to someone by the large fountain to the left of the mansion. The person was standing so close to Tom that Doug later asked Tom who he was "getting close to" by the fountain. Tom said that he hadn't been standing next to anyone near the fountain. Doug swore to Tom that he had seen him standing next to someone, and that explained to Tom the sensation he had experienced of someone standing beside him while he explored the huge fountain area.

I saw some of the wildest shadow people on video while recording in the ballroom on the third floor. It is not known what exactly shadow people are, but they appear as just that: dark, shadowy figures. I was at the mansion for an all-night Halloween event, and it was about 3:30 a.m. We had set up an infrared night-shot camera in the ballroom and sat back to watch if anything would happen on a television monitor in the next room. In the far corner of the ballroom, which is now the restroom at the end of the ballroom, a shadowy figure stepped out from nowhere. Everyone in the room saw it, and we all gasped at the same time. The figure appeared to be humanlike and blacker than the shadows around it. It seemed to be doing a sweeping motion, as if it had a broom, when a second figure appeared next to it. The figures seemed to look at each other, and as quickly as they had appeared, they were both gone. South East Michigan Ghost Hunters were there as well, and everyone tried to re-create the event by standing in the back of the ballroom, seeing if our shadows could have made the movements; but nothing we did equaled what we saw on video. I can remember being so startled by what we were seeing that the hair on my arms stood on end and a chill ran continuously up and down my spine.

The shadows had appeared in a corner where we had a mock graveyard set up, with tombstones and other Halloween props. I had made a couple of tombstones and wasn't keen on walking over to that corner to pick them up when the event was over, even with the lights turned back on. The event was still too fresh in my mind, and I knew that what I had seen was something that couldn't be explained.

A DOOR OPENS BY ITSELF

One night after a ghost tour was finished, Jason Bouchard, then a member of WMGHS, set his video camera on a chair facing Agnes's room on the second floor. I had left by this point, but I do remember very clearly that it was a warm, windless night, and none of the windows in Agnes's room were open. There are heavy French doors leading into a sunroom that overlooks the front of the property. On Jason's video, they open and close once and then really blow open when an old WMGHS member walks into the room. This member was a funny guy, and he remembers saying something inappropriate while cleaning up equipment in the room. All of a sudden, the doors blew open and an icy blast of cool air hit him square on. It was almost as if Agnes was giving him a big old ghostly slap for being crass. Needless to say, it scared the living daylights out of him. Jason's video can be viewed at www.michigansotherside.com.

Nowadays, the Felt Mansion is open for tours, and the restoration is still a work in progress as they continue to restore and fill the house with furniture from the 1920s. The home can also be used for weddings, banquets and private gatherings. Agnes Felt's old bedroom is now the Bride's Room, beautifully decorated and filled with the anticipation of sharing a life with a loved one, something Agnes probably appreciates. Tours are given in the summer and are well worth the visit.

THE LOST SOULS
OF THE *ALPENA*

The sea is rolling as if it were mad.
—Detroit Free Press *in response to the terrible "Alpena Storm"*

Nothing could make you feel more helpless than being at the mercy of Lake Michigan during a storm, and not one single passenger aboard the side-wheel steamer *Alpena*, leaving Grand Haven and bound for Chicago, lived to tell his frightful story. October 15, 1880, was a nice fall day, but the barometer was falling quickly. Three hours into the trip, everything was still fine. The weather was cooperating, but as the night wore on, the winds picked up to gale speeds, and no part of the lake was still. The storm continued to get worse. Over the course of the next two days, the infamous fury of Lake Michigan became known as the Alpena Storm, damaging over ninety ships and possibly taking one hundred lives from the *Alpena* alone, adding to the graveyard at the bottom of the water. To this day, it was one of the worst storms ever seen on Lake Michigan.

Captain Nelson W. Napier had no idea just how bad the storm would become. Napier was a friendly man, well liked by his regular passengers. He had decades of experience on the water and perhaps was overly confident the day he took the *Alpena* out for its last voyage. Wreckage from the *Alpena* washed ashore near Holland, including items with the *Alpena*'s name on them. Bodies started to wash ashore, as well as coffins the ship was carrying as cargo. The ship's flag, a final surrender to the lake, washed ashore in White Lake, Michigan. The entire west coast of Michigan, from as far north as Muskegon down to Saugatuck, was littered with debris from the wreck.

No one knows for sure what happened to the *Alpena*, besides the obvious fact that it was torn apart brutally by the fury of the lake. The bones of the *Alpena* and most of its crew and passengers have never been located. Judging by dead bodies found with stopped watches—all at 10:50 p.m.— it can be assumed that is about the time the ship went under.

Captain Napier's family put up a reward of one hundred dollars for anyone who could find his body, but Lake Michigan kept him for itself, and he was never found. Superstitious sailors have spoken for a long time about seeing a ghost ship trying to make the trip from Grand Haven to Chicago but never succeeding. The *Alpena* is forever doomed to live in the spectral world of Lake Michigan's ghosts.

THE STRANGE TALES
OF THE BEAVER ISLANDS

B eaver Island is a mysterious place with a lot of hidden history that is not common knowledge in every Michigander's head. Ask any local what our state bird is, and he'll say, "A robin!" Ask him about the Mormon King of Beaver Island, and you might get a blank look and a shrug of the shoulders.

Beaver Island rests peacefully in Lake Michigan, twenty miles west of Charlevoix. Home to six hundred people year-round and plenty of tourists in the summer, its picturesque shores and acres of beautiful forest hold secrets that it won't let go. Beaver Island is the largest of twelve sister islands. The first inhabitants of Beaver Island were the Odawas, also known as the Ottawas. Archaeological evidence shows early pottery from the Woodland period, and burial mounds in the harbor area were explored in 1871 by archaeologist Henry Gillman. The island was always a stopping point for people along the trade routes in the days of mass shipping on Lake Michigan. Irish immigrants were some of the first to settle on the island because of its excellent fishing, and it was nicknamed the "Americans' emerald isle." Unlike other islands in Lake Michigan, Beaver Island has the most history and unique stories, creating the perfect elements for a few wandering specters.

Frederick Stonehouse, a prolific Michigan maritime author, points out that he feels that Beaver Island has the "greatest potential for haunting activity. No other area has the history of conflict, trauma and the interplay of people as the Beaver Island area." Stonehouse feels that there have probably been a lot of stories about ghosts and paranormal phenomena on the island, but much of it has gone unreported due to the small population and its remoteness.

History and hauntings are partners in the paranormal. Where there have been traumatic and exciting events, there is usually a haunting or two that goes with it. One could look at it as an island of untouched paranormal potential.

STRANGE, STRANGE STRANG

James Jesse Strang is one of Michigan's lesser-known and more fascinating characters in history. For starters, he was the only man in the United States to ever declare himself a king and to establish a kingdom. Strang was an interesting individual who early on in life had dreams of becoming royalty. According to his diary, he even wanted to find a way to marry into the royal family of England. An intelligent man, Strang held a law degree, had a seat in the Michigan legislature and was a newspaper editor, a Baptist minister and a postmaster, among other miscellaneous jobs that made up his eclectic resume. But everything in James's life changed in 1844, when he met the charismatic leader of the Mormons, Joseph Smith.

Within just a few short months, James was baptized and appointed an elder within the Mormon Church. Strang and Smith hit if off immediately, but when Joseph Smith was assassinated later that same year, a fight for the succession of leadership quickly ensued between James Strang and Brigham Young. Strang argued that he had a letter proving that Joseph Smith had appointed him successor of the church in the event of his death, but Brigham Young, being the more popular of the two, won the argument and was appointed head of the church. Strang, believing that he was the rightful heir and guided by a vision, grabbed what followers he could to start his "heaven on Earth" on Beaver Island in 1848. Eventually, more than two thousand Mormons were living on the island.

Perhaps it started with good intentions, but the final chapter of the Mormon occupation of Beaver Island didn't end well. In the beginning,

Strang condemned the practice of polygamy, but as time went on, Strang took on a secret second wife, Elvira Eliza Field. She traveled beside him dressed as a man and was introduced to people as Charles J. Douglas, Strang's "nephew" and secretary. He eventually encouraged his followers to take on at least a second wife. Strang took on five wives total and fathered fourteen kids by them. At one point, every wife, excluding his first, was pregnant by him.

Strang became more tyrannical and despotic as time went on, and followers soon became haters. Thomas Bedford and another man, Alexander Wentworth, planned the assassination of Strang and succeeded in their mission on June 16, 1856. James died from his wounds on July 9. The two men were never charged with murder; it was believed that the U.S. government had something to do with it. After the assassination, Bedford and Wentworth escaped on the U.S. Navy gunboat *Michigan*, which was docked at Beaver Island. Followers of Strang still exist today, although their numbers are very small.

Following King Strang's death, the Mormons were chased off the island. Strang had reigned for eight years. After his death, many of the original people who fled the island because of the Mormons came back, along with a large migration of Irish people. They found an improved island, with new buildings and a town that was called St. James. The Kings Highway, built by the Mormons on Beaver Island, is still used today.

Is James Strang still king of his island in spirit form? The Old Mormon Print Shop, built in 1850, is the only building left standing from the time of the Mormon occupation. It is now the museum for the Beaver Island Historical Society.

Strang was shot on the shore in front of the shop, and some people claim to have seen his spirit in the area. Given the extreme event of Strang's assassination, it is possible that the area has a residual haunting. Two ghostly men have been spotted in the bushes where Strang was assassinated on multiple occasions. People who have visited the Old Print Shop have felt strange on the second floor, but there is no real evidence of a haunting in the museum.

BEAVER ISLAND LIGHT AND ITS GHOST...
OR LACK THEREOF

Beaver Island Light (also known as Beaver Head) is built on a bluff on the southern end of the island. The first light was built here in 1852, but after several years, the tower collapsed. There doesn't seem to be much information on that particular light. In 1858, the current light was built. The lightkeeper's dwelling was attached to the tower in 1866. The light was discontinued in 1962, and like most of the lights that were taken out of service, it quickly went into disrepair. Weathering and vandalism were destroying the buildings, and the property was considered a lost cause until the Charlevoix Public School District was deeded the land in 1975. Restoration through the years has made this old place beautiful again, and it is now the home of the Beaver Island Lighthouse School. The school helps troubled students graduate from high school. The lighthouse tower is open to the public, so anyone can retrace the steps of the lightkeeper as he traveled up the cast-iron stairs

The Beaver Island Light. *Photo by Kristin Speer.*

daily to maintain the light. The light is on the National Register of Historic Places and can boast being one of the oldest lighthouses on the Great Lakes.

Is there a ghost in the Beaver Head Light Station? Stories have circulated about a ghost being in the light. Phantom footsteps and other strange disturbances have been heard on the tower stairs and on the second floor, but nothing major. Students at the Beaver Lighthouse School have talked about a ghost, but kids will talk, and when it comes to spooky stuff, they will talk even more! A former teacher at the Beaver Island Lighthouse School said that the students spent a night in the light one night and couldn't even make it through the entire night. They were too spooked! For now, it seems, this is just ghostly speculation, but what would a lighthouse be without its ghost?

THE ENIGMATIC PROTAR

If you have ever just wanted to get away from it all, Beaver Island is the place for you and for a mysterious man by the name of Feodor Protar, who lived on the island from 1893 until his death in 1925. During his time on the island, Protar's status among his fellow islanders was near saint like, and he gained the recognition and respect of anyone who met him. If said in two syllables with a robot-like voice, the name "Pro-Tar" sounds like it's from another planet, but it would seem that Protar was, in fact, a "heaven-sent friend," as the inscription on his tombstone implies. He was known as "Dr. Protar" to the islanders, and he spent his final years helping his fellow islanders with simple remedies and folk cures when they weren't feeling well. Old photos of Protar show him sporting a bushy, Santa-like beard and long white hair—a cross between Santa Claus and Walt Whitman, two people who shared similar characteristics with Protar.

Traveling the Great Lakes, Protar was introduced to Beaver Island after a storm forced him to dock his boat there. Something about the island resonated with him, and he started to vacation there regularly. On one of his trips, he found an old, empty log cabin, inquired about it and became owner of two hundred acres of land and the cabin. Like a hippie ahead of his time, Protar lived off the land, let his hair and beard grow long and even kept a diary of daily weather on the island. He was a mystery when he arrived and stayed a mystery for the rest of his life. No one questioned his origins or bothered him. He even went as far as to hide his real last name. "Protar" was an anagram for his real last name: Parrot. His neighbors knew he preferred to keep to himself. He was essentially a hermit from the moment he set foot on the island. But Protar was kind and always there to help anyone in need of his assistance or advice, especially poor people who couldn't afford the doctor in the island's town of St. James.

Protar's biographer, Anje Price, spent a considerable amount of time researching who the real Protar was. Born in Russia around 1838, Protar came from an educated family of doctors and scientists. Protar

Protar's tomb on Beaver Island. *Photo by Kristin Speer.*

had also studied medicine for a time, hence the reason he was able to give simple medical advice. Legends and stories circulated while he was still alive. Some people have speculated in the past that Protar was running from the Russian government and was in some type of exile due to his mysterious nature, but Price feels that he was running from the "man within." He was looking for a simple and spiritual life. One of his strongest beliefs was the old saying, "Better to give than to receive." Price wrote that Protar was "a haunted, hunted, desperate man," and he seemed to be his own worst critic.

On the night before his death, a passage in one of his books was marked; it read, "The only preparation for death is a virtuous life." Had Protar sensed the end coming? Ironically, one of Protar's closest friends (who no doubt knew the secrets behind the man), Dr. Carl Bernhardi, died on the very same day as Protar, both men taking their secrets to the grave. It was Protar's wish to be buried at sea, but laws prevented that from happening. The island people built a tomb and monument for him, inscribing it, "to our heaven-sent friend…who never failed us. In imperishable gratitude and admiration, his people of Beaver Island." Feodor Protar was so highly respected that some speculate they buried him at sea anyway and put up the monument so that no one suspected they had broken the law. To this day, Protar's spirit is felt on the island that he so loved. He is now part of the land and the spiritual world with which he was trying to become one. Protar's old cabin can be visited and is on the National Register of Historic Places.

THE MYSTERIOUS STONE CIRCLE OF BEAVER ISLAND

Beaver Island is home to a mysterious set of stones. There are thirty-nine stones in total, creating a 397-foot circle. The stones vary in size, and how the stones got there is the biggest mystery of all. Most assume that it was done by the Native Americans. The stones were found in 1985 by Terry Bussey, who was looking for Native American artifacts and found something she wasn't planning on discovering. When she came upon the scattered stones, something told her that they weren't

The largest stone in the Beaver Island Stone Circle. Offerings are now placed in the center of it. *Photo by Kristin Speer.*

placed there by nature. There seemed to be a pattern, and some stones appeared to have been hand carved. Bussey used a compass, spent a couple nights under the stars with the stones and noticed that the stones connect to star positions. Later research found that the stones were aligned to the midsummer solstice.

Some archaeologists shrug off the stones as nothing, while others speculate that they were placed by the Mound Builders thousands of years ago or the more recent Native Americans who inhabited the island for so long.

There are smaller groups of circles that have been added to for spiritual purposes, and the pattern of the stones is similar to that of a Native American medicine wheel. The thing that perplexes archaeologists about the stones is the fact that the bands of Native Americans living in that area didn't usually create stone monuments. So who placed the stones, and what were they for? There is a lot to be learned about Michigan's ancient history.

HIDDEN TREASURE OF THE MORMON KINGDOM

There is a story told about hidden treasure that was buried on High Island when the Mormons were being kicked off the island after Strang was killed. As treasurer and "king" of the island, Strang took it upon himself to be the sole keeper of the kingdom's wealth. It was expected of the followers to give a tithe, as Mormons still do today. On the day that Strang was shot, one of his loyal followers went to retrieve the money hidden away and carried it to a cabin west of town in St. James. Under the light of the moon, the box was quietly taken away on a boat and rowed over to nearby High Island. The man ran to a spot not far from the shore and buried the box safely in the ground.

Since that time, the island has been stripped of its trees for lumber, and it is not known whether the treasure was found or even if it had ever really been buried on High Island. The box of cash could still be buried somewhere out there, but odds are that the secret is long sealed away with dead lips.

High Island was also home to the House of David sect, from Benton Harbor, which arrived in 1912 after its leader, Benjamin Purnell, purchased the High Island lumber company. These memorable people were best known for the men's long hair, which they never cut, their excellent traveling baseball team and their belief that they would live for one thousand years. Benjamin Purnell also went by the title "king." The House of David eventually fell apart after the government came after Purnell on morality charges. The members living on High Island were gone by the 1940s, and no traces of their existence remain on the island, except, perhaps, the graves of their dead, which were never marked since they were supposed to live one thousand years.

When it comes to ghosts and colorful characters on Beaver Island, there is no doubt to many people who study Michigan maritime history that the islands have seen tons of fascinating history. In fact, Frederick Stonehouse points out in his work that "if there's any place on Lake Michigan that has ghosts, Beaver Island has to have its share of them."

THE GHOSTS OF THE *IRONSIDES*

Could the spirits of the old shipwrecked *Ironsides*, about four miles from Grand Haven's coast, still be lost in the waters of Lake Michigan? The *Ironsides* was a beautiful steamer first launched in 1864. Its black twin smokestacks, white painted woodwork and graceful support arches on both sides of the boat gave the ship that old-fashioned look not seen any more on the big lakes. Perhaps it was a bad omen when its sister ship, the *Lac la Belle*, sank to Lake Michigan's bottom near Racine, Wisconsin, on October 14, 1872. One year later, and just nine years after its first launch on the water on September 15, 1873, the *Ironsides* sailed for the last time on Lake Michigan.

During 1873, the *Ironsides* was given a thorough inspection. Anything that needed repair got it, and the ship was thought to be in excellent shape for travel, although it seemed to have some phantom leaks that worried the captain and the crew. On September 15, what was a normal breeze turned into gale winds that swept over Lake Michigan. As the ship approached its Grand Haven destination, Captain Harry Sweetman tried to navigate it toward the Grand Haven channel. It was a losing battle as the turbulent waves and wind enveloped Lake Michigan in a menacing storm. Coming dangerously close to Grand Haven's beach, the ship struck ground a few times, causing the hull to start taking on water. According to reports from divers who have visited the underwater wreck, the propellers are tangled, and there was, in fact, a hole in the ship's hull. Water entering the hull would have extinguished the fires of the boiler, leaving the ship powerless to propel itself out of the terrible storm.

As the morning hours approached, all hope was lost, and no options seemed available to the doomed passengers and crew. About 11:00 a.m., the ship's five lifeboats were dropped into the upset water in an attempt to escape the inevitable sinking of the ship. The famous line, "A captain goes down with the ship," is true in the case of the *Ironsides*, as Harry Sweetman made sure that the crew and passengers were all safely on lifeboats before he thought of himself. Of the five lifeboats, only two of them barely made it to Grand Haven's shore. The other three lifeboats met their demise, as did Captain Sweetman. The exact number of deaths isn't known, but it is estimated that anywhere from twenty to thirty people perished that night.

Wreckage and other debris, along with dead bodies, washed ashore on Grand Haven's beach. The topic was widely reported in the *Grand Haven Tribune* and other papers. An old *New York Times* article from September 17, 1873, reported, "The ladies of Grand Haven took charge of the bodies and saw them properly…coffined." The bodies were stored and put on ice at the D&M Railroad Depot (currently one of the Tri-Cities Historical Museums), which was used as a temporary morgue for the victims.

Paranormal theories suggest that traumatic events leave behind impressions. It is as if the events get recorded into the atmosphere and, if the conditions are right, can be replayed. The residual energy left behind from the traumatic sinking of the *Ironsides* might have replayed itself for the United States Coast Guard in 2000, when coast guardsmen encountered a strange voice on the waters just past Grand Haven's pier.

The Coast Guard icebreaker *Mackinaw* was leaving the annual Grand Haven Coast Guard Festival on August 6, 2000. As the ship moved out into Lake Michigan, the night's fog slowly crept around the ship. Now, every good ghost story needs to start with some fog, and the *Mackinaw* found itself slipping into its very own ghost story.

As the ship watched the lights of Grand Haven's pier twinkle behind it in the distance, the crew onboard suddenly heard the distressed voice of a little boy calling for help. Everyone on deck was certain about the voice, and not having any luck finding the little boy in the fog, they radioed back to Grand Haven for a search party. Michigan maritime author Wes Oleszewski pointed out when he first reported this story

90

The Ghosts of the *Ironsides*

The *Ironsides*. *Photo courtesy of the Loutit District Library.*

that for the Coast Guard to send out extra help pre–September 11, when its budget was paper thin, meant that the voice the crew heard was no joke. The Coast Guard continued to search, asking passing boaters if they had heard or seen anything. All of them said no, and no little boy was found. Paranormal stories or experiences from people are sometimes taken with a grain of salt. We have no way of backing them up or proving them in a scientific lab, but when a paranormal story comes from the U.S. Coast Guard, it's rather hard to ignore.

Could an old article in the *New York Times* from September 16, 1873, offer a clue to the mystery of the little boy's phantom voice? The article reported a chilling description of a little boy who was found dead. Maybe it is an insight into the ghostly voice the Coast Guard heard that August evening:

> *The little boy of Mrs. Valentine, whose body came ashore, was dressed in a sailor's suit of blue, had light hair, blue eyes, and beautiful features, and with the exception of paleness to the face looked as though he had dropped quietly to his last sleep. It was a scene that would have touched*

the hardest heart to see the sorrow-stricken husband and father who arrived from Milwaukee this morning, when he recognized his wife and the little boy, and knew that his whole family had been so suddenly taken from him forever.

Bob Beaton, a historian from West Michigan, has researched other interesting stories about the *Ironsides*. Bob said that the wreck has a "few mysteries and odd occurrences" attached to it. One of the surviving crewmembers was being interviewed about the incident. The crewmember was very "free" in telling his story until he realized that the man he was talking to was a newspaper reporter. According to Bob:

He then shut up as though he had something to hide. It may have had something to do with a crewmember or a portion of the crew not acting in an honorable way regarding the passengers when the lifeboats overturned on the sandbars near shore.

Bob mentioned two other eerie scenes from that tragic day. The first was the deeply sad site of a married couple on their honeymoon washed ashore on Grand Haven's beach, dead but still in an embrace. The man's name was Harry Hasebarth. The other disturbing image was of a lifeboat overturned in the water. Bob's research found that a man went up to the boat, tugged on a rope that was attached to it and found a body attached to that rope. It was the body of the ship's stewardess that had been tied to the floor of the lifeboat. What had happened during the chaos of the storm and the ship beginning to sink that provoked such a gruesome act as tying someone to the bottom of a boat?

Years after the boat sank, its mast stuck out above the water as an eerie reminder of the lives lost. It was one of the worst days in Grand Haven's history in terms of loss of life. The location of the wreck was forgotten with time, until two divers, in 1966, rediscovered it. The site is now protected as a historical dive site and is considered an advanced dive.

Are the spirits of the deceased who died during the *Ironsides* still restless? Do their ghosts still wander the old wreck, trying to figure out what happened to them? If you're ever in the area of the *Ironsides*, keep your eyes and ears peeled for mysterious voices and maybe even a ghostly glimpse of the ship still trying to escape the storm that sent it, and many others, to its grave.

LEGENDS AND GHOSTS
OF MOUTH CEMETERY

Number 6666 Sunset Lane? Sounds like the perfect place for a ghost story…or a haunted cemetery. The historic Mouth Cemetery, well hidden in the woods of Montague, is host to legends and ghost stories galore. A small, one-lane road leads you back to the iron-gated cemetery, haphazardly scattered with old, and a few new, tombstones. A large white sign with black letters reads "Mouth Cemetery," with the hours noted as 8:00 a.m. to 8:00 p.m. An old, dilapidated wooden shack rests to the left of the cemetery, littered with old cars, furniture and other debris. The black iron gate, once adorned with horse heads long since vandalized and gone, gives the clichéd creaking sound as it is pushed open.

The ground is mossy and squishy to walk on in parts, creating the feeling that your foot might sink below the surface at any moment into something unimaginable. Even during the day, there is a stillness there that's hard to explain unless you visit the old burial grounds. It is easy to see how so many ghost stories are told about the place, especially once the sun sets and the only light available is the overhead security light near the cemetery gates, no doubt creating an eerie glow over the tombstones that dwell near it.

At over 150 years old, Mouth Cemetery is the oldest burial ground in White Lake Township, the oldest grave dating to 1851. While the cemetery seems remote by today's standards, it was once located by the first settlement of the area in the 1840s called the White River Village. A plaque commemorating the cemetery's history reads, "The cemetery is the resting place for Indians, early settlers, children of Revolutionary

The front gates of
Mouth Cemetery.
*Photo by Amberrose
Hammond.*

War soldiers and shipwrecked sailors. Many graves are unmarked or
marked with wooden crosses now gone."

A local resident, Megan Aspiranti, is no stranger to the paranormal.
Megan knew that she was sensitive to the other side and strange
moments in her life affirmed that feeling. A former fiancé was taking
her through Montague and Newaygo, showing her places where he
had grown up. Megan began seeing flashes and streaks of red that
she knew weren't really there. Driving down to the next block, they
came upon an old abandoned house, badly falling apart. Her fiancé
told her that a family had been murdered there. Had Megan been
picking up on the terrible past events in the area? Megan feels that
she was. When friends wanted to visit the Mouth Cemetery for a
good scare at night, Megan joined them, making it her first trip to the

burial ground. Her friends all believed that the place was haunted, having heard creepy stories about the place for years, but Megan had her doubts. She asked her husband about Mouth before going, and he stated, "If there was a haunted cemetery in Montague, that would be it."

One of the main attractions in Mouth Cemetery is the "devil's chair." Like most cemetery tales, elements of folklore have sunk into Mouth along with the crooked tombstones. Devil's chairs are a popular cemetery legend that can be found all over the county. The story typically says that if a person sits in one of these chairs, they are bound to die soon, will see their death or will get a personal visit from the devil himself. Many of the stories started with the old benches placed near tombstones in Victorian times, when mourning for the dead was taken very seriously. The chairs eventually got a reputation, and before you knew it, they were the property of the devil.

Wandering into the dark cemetery, Megan's friends led her to a chair near some tombstones. The original chair had been replaced with a much newer one, but that didn't matter. The new one was cursed as well. Megan was told "that you would die one year from the day, hour and minute that you sat in it." Defying what the legend and her friends told her, Megan took a seat in the chair, feeling that it was nothing more than a silly story. She's still alive to tell her tale today and doubts that her "eventual death will be in anyway related to that chair." She further states, for the record, "The cemetery did not feel even the least bit haunted. I believe the fear was created by people scaring themselves." If you visit Mouth, will you take a seat in the devil's chair? Just as a precaution, maybe it's better to just admire the chair from afar and not risk it.

On the other side of the coin, a few very objective people have come away from the cemetery with stories that they could not explain. Jennifer, a native of west Michigan, is a completely objective person. She knows that many of the photos trying to be passed off as paranormal "orbs" are nothing more than dust, and she knows that a lot of paranormal experiences had by people are a result of over-active imaginations on a midnight jaunt in a spooky place. It was Devil's Night the first time Jennifer visited Mouth Cemetery with a group of friends.

Legends and Ghosts of Mouth Cemetery

She had heard scary stories about Mouth and was looking forward to visiting the cemetery. On her first night there, she was with six friends checking out the cemetery. The night was pitch black, and it was long before the security light was set in place. Her friends had talked about the legendary devil's chair, only they spoke of it as the Sadony chair, a chair that the Montague mystic Joseph Sadony had personally cursed himself.

The chair doesn't exist in the cemetery but is located some distance out in the woods, off the Mouth property. Local legend says that if you sat in the Sadony chair, you would die on the seventh of something. It could be the seventh month, the seventh day, the seventh hour or the seventh second, but it would be the number seven that would be the end of you. Jennifer was too scared to visit the chair, and while friends took off to find the elusive chair, she preferred to wait outside the cemetery gates and admire the spooky place from afar. "As long as I was outside of the gates, I felt fine. But it was within the gates that I got scared," Jennifer said. Jennifer questioned whether it was psychological, but either way, she felt something in the place that she couldn't deny. That was when she had her first, and very real, paranormal experience.

Standing outside the gates, not even within the cemetery itself, she saw an orange-colored ball of light form in the trees. It hovered above the cemetery. She yelled for everyone to come forward to look, and it vanished. Her friend told her that it was nothing and she was just getting herself worked up. That's when the light appeared for a second time, hovering in the trees, only to blink out again. It came back a third time to allow the others to see it too. Everyone was stunned and couldn't explain what they were seeing. Was it the long lost spirit of someone buried within the cemetery, or perhaps a long-departed Native American spirit still keeping watch over the burial grounds that belonged to them first? Either way, more than one person witnessed the light that night, and no one could explain where it came from.

Angie Berg, a paranormal investigator from Grand Haven, first heard about Mouth Cemetery from her teenage niece and nephew, who had heard stories at school about strange things happening there. Tales of everything from a glowing tombstone, crying children and bizarre photos were being whispered among the kids. After hearing this, Angie, having always been interested in the paranormal but also a skeptic, drove out to Mouth Cemetery the day after Halloween 2003. She had visited the cemetery before for its historical value but had never heard about it being haunted. There were no glowing headstones or crying children, but something about the cemetery drew her in:

> It's now my favorite cemetery to visit. It is back in the woods. Lake Michigan is just over the ridge, and it is very quiet out there. There are times we have been out there and the air is super-charged. You can feel the energy in the air. Other times, it is peaceful. This is an area where I can still "feel" the history. I have a feeling that something is going to happen every time I visit.

Before the settlers in the area began putting their dead in the grounds of Mouth Cemetery, local Native Americans used the plot.

Quismoqua Anderson's tombstone, Mouth Cemetery. *Photo by Amberrose Hammond.*

While walking through the cemetery, one can't help but notice the mounds in many places in the perfect shape of a burial, some marked by crosses and many more not marked at all. It is widely known that Native Americans chose their burial places for specific reasons, usually because there was a special connection with the land or a certain energy that attracted them. Many feel that these places were chosen because they were places where the dead could make a smooth transition into the next life.

One of the most popular Native American gravestones to locate is that of Quismoqua Anderson, an Ottawa women who lived to be 110 years old. Because of her age, her tombstone has always attracted attention, and some even feel that her spirit may be around as well. People still honor her grave by placing Native American objects, such as dream catchers, near it.

THE GHOST OF CAPTAIN WILLIAM ROBINSON AND THE WHITE RIVER LIGHTHOUSE STATION

The first lightkeeper of the nearby White River Light Station has a final resting place toward the back of Mouth Cemetery, overlooking the water he always helped keep safe. William Robinson was buried in Mouth Cemetery in 1919. Ghost stories say that Captain William Robinson has ghostly dual citizenship in Mouth Cemetery and his beloved lighthouse. Lighthouse keepers back in the day took their jobs very seriously. It was up to them to guide ships around dangerous waters and to steer them safely into harbors. If a lightkeeper didn't do his job, many lives could be lost. Perhaps that's why you hear about so many lighthouses being haunted by their old keepers. And perhaps that's why William Robinson still watches over the light and the people who come to visit every year.

The White River Light Station was built in 1875. It was automated in 1945 and put out of use in 1960. Fruitland Township bought the property in 1966 and began using it as a park. The lighthouse was restored and opened in 1970 as a museum. Captain Robinson first served at the South Pierhead Light in 1871. When the time came to

Captain William Robinson's grave in Mouth Cemetery. *Photo by Amberrose Hammond.*

build the White River Light nearby, Robinson oversaw the building of the light and took over as lightkeeper when it was finished. A legend while alive, being the oldest keeper on active duty before he retired, his legacy continues after his death.

William Robinson devoted forty-seven years of his life to the lighthouse and was forced out of his position due to age, but the lighthouse was his duty in life. Robinson and his wife raised their large family at the light, and when his wife, Sarah, died before him, taking care of the light became even more important to distract his thoughts from missing her terribly. Captain Robinson's oldest grandson took over as the next lightkeeper, but due to government regulations, only the lightkeeper and his immediate family were allowed to live at the light. Sadly, Captain Robinson had to finally leave his home after four decades of dedicated service. William told his grandson, "I am not going to leave the building," and it has been said that he died the day he was supposed to leave. His stubbornness has carried on in his next life, as it seems that the second

The White River Light Station. *Photo by Tom Maat.*

floor of the White River Light Station is literally his stomping grounds in the afterlife; footsteps can occasionally be heard.

Karen McDonnell has been the curator of what is now the White River Light Station Museum for over twenty years. A reporter for the *Muskegon Chronicle* interviewed Karen McDonnell for an article about the lighthouse. She doesn't claim that the lighthouse has any bona fide ghosts or extreme paranormal moments at every corner. What she does admit to, though, are phantom footsteps on the second floor, receiving a brief flash of a couple looking out the top-story window in the tower, footsteps in the lighthouse stairwell, a light blinking strangely in the light room and the feeling that Captain William Robinson and his wife, Sarah, are still around.

McDonnell relayed a wonderful story to author Frederick Stonehouse about her experience with the second ghost of the lighthouse, Sarah Robinson, the captain's wife. After finding some photos of Sarah, Karen decided to place them on display. She couldn't help but think how happy Captain Robinson would be to have photos of his beloved wife back up in the lighthouse. While cleaning a glass case that always needs cleaning, Karen put down her dust rag and went to answer the phone that was ringing. When she came back upstairs to finish cleaning the case, the case had been perfectly wiped down, and the rag was on the opposite side from where she had left it. Did Sarah come back and clean the case for her as a thank-you from beyond the grave? Karen stated that she would leave the rag on the case and walk away on purpose, always to find the case clean and the rag moved.

The ghosts are not frightening to the curator; she is comforted that there's always someone looking out for her and the lighthouse.

THE MYSTERIOUS JOSEPH SADONY

Next door to Mouth Cemetery lies an old, rickety-looking wooden shack that local talk says belonged to the Montague mystic Joseph Sadony. His studies in using intuition are not well known and are extremely fascinating. He believed that everyone had intuition that they could use to their advantage, but they just had to learn how to properly "tune" into it. He believed that psychic powers and intuition were very scientific processes, and there was nothing "supernatural" about the phenomena.

Joseph was born in Mountbauer, Germany, on February 22, 1877. He moved to Kalamazoo with his parents in 1884.

Joseph's granddaughter, Jennifer Sadony Westrate, in a *Muskegon Chronicle* article from 2005, remembered, "When some people saw grandpa coming, they would cross the street. Grandpa said things that would scare them. They were afraid he could read their minds." According to the article, Sadony made over thirty-eight thousand accurate predictions in his time. Even the Chicago and Detroit Police Departments kept Joseph handy for those hard-to-crack cases.

One could say that Joseph Sadony had a knack for extrasensory perception. He was keenly aware of his intuition and how to properly use it. He was never a showoff and didn't use his abilities to impress anyone. He might have even been instrumental in saving a ship on Lake Michigan that was about to become the next "ghost ship."

Another devastating storm had hit Lake Michigan, and the schooner *Our Son* was caught out on the open water. The ship might have already been cursed from its beginnings in 1875, when the shipbuilder's son fell into the water near the new ship and drowned. Captain Henry Kelley, the builder, named the boat *Our Son* in honor of him.

The *Our Son* was one of the last lumber ships to sail Lake Michigan and made its last stop to Muskegon on September 26, 1930. While leaving port, the ship soon found itself twenty miles outside of Ludington in a wicked storm. The ship was fifty-five years old, and its old bones couldn't take the gale-force winds. The sails were torn to pieces, and waves crashed into the ship, causing the boat to start taking on water. Captain Fred Nelson sent up the distress flag, but how would anyone ever see his ship in the horrible weather? It looked as though the crew had met its end.

Another ship, the *William Nelson*, sailed by Captain Charles Mohr, was traveling in the storm south from Mackinac. Captain Mohr should have docked his ship in a port somewhere, but for some reason, he kept his boat moving, sustaining damage the whole way. Mohr was no stranger to saving lives on the Great Lakes, having saved four other ships in the past. There was something telling him that his help was strongly needed near Ludington. As he approached the area, he saw the *Our Son*, barely afloat on the water. Captain Mohr got his ship close enough for the crew of seven to jump overboard onto the *William Nelson*.

Was it psychic intuition that brought Captain Mohr to the aid of the *Our Son*? Joseph Sadony was watching the turbulent rise and fall of Lake Michigan from his home in Montague. Talking with friends, they wondered if there were any ships stuck out on the water. Joseph stated that there was, in fact, a ship in dire need of help, and if the captain of another ship nearby trusted his intuition, all would be saved. Ironically, Joseph Sadony and Charles Mohr were friends, and once Mohr found out that his old friend had "seen" their ships out on the storm, there was no doubt in his mind that the psychic connection he and his friend shared helped save the crew of the *Our Son*.

Sadony was hard to put a finger on. Even his close friends couldn't always describe the man who was a mystery in his own community. In recent years, his family has been striving to restore his Valley of the Pines and to bring back his teachings and memory. The Valley of the Pines was eighty acres of beautiful, wooded land purchased in 1906 by Joseph. Joseph bought the Valley of the Pines in order to "develop…a center of psychological research and investigation into the realms of the physical sciences," according to his obituary. Like in Mouth Cemetery, there seems to be something special about the land in the area—a peaceful feeling that emanates all around.

THE MISSING BODIES OF
THE CURSED *CHICORA*

Here's a sigh for the Chicora, *for the broken, sad* Chicora.
Here's a tear for those who followed her beneath the tossing wave.
O the mystery of the morrow—from its shadows let us borrow
A star of hope to shine above the gloom of every grave.
                                                    —*Nixon Waterman*

When sailors saw the ghost ship of the *Chicora*, glimpsing it through a foggy haze on the water, it meant that the crew was in for some rough times. The *Chicora* became a bad omen on the lake, and the men took caution, fearing what was in store for them. Built in 1892, the *Chicora* had a cruising speed of seventeen miles per hour and was over two hundred feet long. Its main purpose was to bring passengers and goods back and forth from Milwaukee to St. Joseph, Michigan. The ship had fifty-six luxury rooms for higher-class citizens with money to live first-class lifestyles on the boat, and there were regular rooms for the average, everyday person. The ship was "luxuriously furnished," complete with mahogany wood and electric lighting.

The *Chicora* was sailed by Edward G. Stines, who had more than two decades of sailing experience on the Great Lakes. Before it was to set sail on the day of its final journey, Captain Stines was told not to sail by his doctor. He had been sick, and the doctor advised him to stay home and rest before getting back to his job. Figuring that he was in a fine condition to sail and that the journey would be an easy one, he ignored the doctor's orders. This was the first sign the good captain didn't bother to notice that could have saved his life and the lives of the passengers. The second bad omen was brought on by a man named Joseph Pearl, traveling to Milwaukee from St. Joseph on the *Chicora*. A duck had appeared out of nowhere in the middle of the lake. The bird was considered a strange sign, and the superstitious captain heralded it as a sign of bad luck—even more so when the man from St. Joseph shot it down with a gun he had brought with him.

Joseph bragged to Captain Stines about his marksmanship, and it was described in a *Milwaukee Sentinel* article that the captain "began to turn pale" and exclaimed to Joseph, "My God, Pearl, what have you done? I feel like kneeling down and praying." From that point on, the entire crew was in a depressed state, already feeling the fate that was near. The story about the duck began to spread rapidly. Soon, it was being said that the duck was an "immense gull," and the *Michigan City Dispatch*, on January 31, days after the *Chicora* went missing, published that "there is a superstition among sailors that 'ill-luck follows him who kills a seagull.'" Many of the crewmembers refused to travel back toward St. Joseph with Joseph Pearl onboard, but they most likely were assured by others that "they were being silly and superstitious." Author Kit Lane, in his book *Chicora: Lost on Lake Michigan*, writes that "in the distant past it was linked to the idea that drowned men were reincarnated as seabirds and that killing one was tantamount to killing a shipmate and evil luck would surely follow."

Nevertheless, Captain Stines, ignoring the doctor's orders to rest and trying to forget about the duck, set the *Chicora* to sail on Monday, January 21, 1895, toward St. Joseph from Milwaukee, with passengers and flour that was in high demand onboard. This ship's usual second mate was sick, and to replace him, Captain Stiles brought on his twenty-three-year-old son. The weather was nice for a winter's day and was described as being "spring like." There were no signs that it would change. The steamer didn't usually run that late in the season, but there was a high demand for the flour it was carrying as cargo, so the owners no doubt felt that it was worth the trip. Ten minutes after the *Chicora* set sail, a message arrived a few minutes too late, telling the captain to stay docked as the barometer was falling fast in Benton Harbor, Michigan, a sure sign of a storm brewing.

The Missing Bodies of the Cursed *Chicora*

Lake Michigan is very unpredictable, and before captain and crew knew it, the lake had whipped up one of its finest storms. Massive waves crashed into the sides of the *Chicora*, and the winds blew fierce and fast. The storm lasted for two days. John H. Graham, one of the owners of the *Chicora*, had a house in St. Joseph with a tower on its roof. He sat within the tower, one of the highest points in St. Joseph, scanning the waters in hopes of glimpsing the *Chicora*. Rumors that people spotted it a couple miles off the coast of St. Joseph surfaced, but the blizzard conditions made it near impossible to see anything for certain. Friends and family eagerly awaited the ship's return in St. Joseph. All ports along the southwest coast of Michigan were alerted to be on the lookout for the doomed *Chicora*. Even Captain Stines's brother, Henry, was in his steamer *City of Ludington*, searching desperately.

When the first bits of wreckage started to wash ashore at Saugatuck and farther north, people knew that the *Chicora* had met its match. Pieces of the ship, and even furniture, started to appear. A search party was formed and, along with other ships, combed the waters and the shore, but no bodies were ever found. According to the *Great Lakes Journal* from 1919, a skeleton hand was found hanging onto a hat with the initials "G&M" years later. G&M stood for the *Chicora*'s company owners, Graham and Morton Transportation Co, but no one knew if the skeleton story was true or just a legend.

To this day, the *Chicora* is one of Lake Michigan's biggest mysteries when it comes to shipwrecks. Rumors circulated during the month after its sinking that a floating hull was found, with crewmembers of the *Chicora* alive and clinging for their lives to the battered wood. According to the Michigan Shipwrecks website:

> *During the first week in February, a Chicago-based tug reported sighting a hulk floating on the open water with crew members still alive! W.J. Hancock, regular clerk of the* Chicora *who missed the sailing, was sent to the southern part of the lake to investigate. After renting a tug he reported seeing only a dark iceberg covered with seagulls.*

All kinds of crazy stories started to be told about the disappearance of the *Chicora*. Two of the most intriguing ones were of bottles found with messages inside from the crew of the cursed ship. On April 14, a bottle came ashore with a message reading, "All is lost, could see land if not snowed and blowed. Engine give out, drifting to shore in ice. Captain and clerk are swept off. We have a hard time of it. 10:15 o'clock." A week later, a second bottle washed up in Glencoe, Illinois, with a small note written on notebook paper that read, "*Chicora* engines broke. Drifted into trough of sea. We have lost all hope. She has gone to pieces. Good bye. McClure, Engineer." People speculate whether the notes were real or just a hoax, but either way, they are a creepy reminder of what the crew went through. At least twenty-three men went down with the ship, and no bodies were ever found. It is believed that they still man the *Chicora*, now part of another realm, appearing to other ships to warn them of dangers to come.

A POSSESSION IN
MUSKEGON COUNTY

AUTHOR'S PERSONAL GHOST STORY

Not all stories are old legends with tons of history to back them up. Some are new legends waiting to be born, with the history currently in the making. There are moments in paranormal investigation that make one consider things very carefully, and this story was one of those moments. Possession had always felt very "Hollywood" to me, and I figured that a lot of the spooky aspects that came along with it were generated by special effects in movies and a good makeup department. There were no such things as animated corpses rising from the grave, demons crawling in dark corners or little girls who were able to spin their head around 360 degrees. That stuff was all nonsense and didn't really happen.

Our small group of paranormal investigators for Michigan's Otherside wasn't ready for the strange events that would unfold one night in September 2003. We had been invited to check out a business in Muskegon County. (The business and location will go unnamed to protect the current owners from any unwanted attention.)

The shop owners had been experiencing strange things. Objects in the store would turn up missing, only to appear somewhere else in the store later on. Most of their electronics had numerous malfunctions, including their security cameras. They had a man come in and look at the cameras, and he couldn't find one thing wrong with the system. In addition, their back office computer went through multiple monitors. Right next to the office was a large storage area. It was from that storage area that the shop owners got major "creeps," as if something was always back there watching them. One of the owners constantly turned around to see if there was someone standing behind her.

What is interesting about this case is the fact that the building was brand-new. It wasn't your stereotypical haunted building from the 1800s. There wasn't any history to be researched about the building; there was nothing but the empty land on which it was built. So does that mean whatever was haunting their store was attached to the land?

I walked into the investigation not expecting much to happen. We wanted to help figure out why the owners were experiencing all of these strange things, but without any building history or other clues, it was going to be a game of "sit and wait." Other investigators had already arrived on location and set up basic equipment: video cameras, thermometers and EMF (electromagnetic field) detectors. Shortly after the investigation began, the EMF detectors started going off at alarming rates that we had never seen before, especially considering one detector only detects natural sources of EMF and nothing man-made, such as computers or electrical wiring. For hours we dealt with bizarre jumps on our meters and even missing objects. While taking a break, I let the shop owner know that I wanted to buy something from the store. I placed the object on the counter and went to my bag for my wallet. When I looked up again, the object was gone. No one had been near me or behind the counter. The owner found the object clear across the other side of the front counter on the floor. That incident took place in a matter of minutes.

While all of our equipment was responding to the environment in bizarre ways, we were in no way ready for the night's final event. Investigators Tom Maat and Nikki Ashendorf were sitting near each other in the storage room when Nikki said, "I don't feel so good...something doesn't feel right." Nikki held her head down and did in fact look a little weak. At that same time, something in the room felt different, similar to that feeling one gets before a thunderstorm arrives. The air felt thick and charged, and that's when something went wrong with Nikki.

Nikki suddenly lurched forward toward Tom, arms outstretched as if reaching to grasp hold of his body. Everyone in the room jumped back. Something was wrong. Nikki lurched toward Tom again, each time slumping back. Her movements were jerky, as if she was on a marionette string and not in control of her own muscles. Tom grabbed hold of her and she snapped out of it. The scary event only lasted a few minutes, but Nikki has no recollection of it to this day. She felt sick afterward, and dizzy, but quickly recovered to her normal self. Nikki has been clairvoyant all of her life, receiving strange messages from the other side at unexpected moments, sometimes seeing spirits and, in this case, experiencing a spirit possession.

What we saw that night led me to rethink my position on a lot of my former beliefs. I no longer felt that a lot of the stuff we were exploring was just "fluff." There was a darker side to it that I didn't know existed.

THE MURDER AND
GHOST OF KATE KOOPMAN

Whether it is the ghost of the victim searching for justice or just trying to find peace, there's something about a thoughtless and vicious crime that keeps a spirit bound to this world. History has a way of burying itself, and in the case of the white brick home on Fulton Street, the murder that took place there in 1922 slipped through the cracks. The stories and facts became buried in old newspapers, left to become nothing more than rumor and urban legend.

Stephanie, a lifelong resident of Grand Haven, used to hear from her grandmother that "an axe murder had happened at the old home long ago" and that the house was possibly haunted. That's all anybody ever really heard, she said. When Linda Forbes and a friend came into the library where I work with questions concerning ghosts, a possible murder and the haunted house Linda owned, the reference librarian found me and asked if I'd be willing to talk to Linda. I came out and greeted Linda, who introduced herself as the owner of Second Impression, a consignment shop at 310 Fulton. She had heard rumors about a murder in the home's past but didn't know for sure. Linda and her co-workers, past and present, had all felt and heard strange things in the old 1800s home. I was startled and excited at the same time. What if there was actually some truth to the rumors I had always heard?

We ventured into the library's local history room and started on a search for some house history. Luckily, Jeanette Weiden, Loutit's local history specialist, knew a little something to get us started in the right direction. Someone had brought a mirror into the local history department that

The outdoor sign for Second Impression consignment shop. *Photo by Amberrose Hammond.*

had once belonged to the Eagle Saloon in Grand Haven. The bar was owned by Peter Koopman, who had been convicted of killing his wife and had lived at 310 Fulton. Intrigued by a small-town murder mystery, I spent weeks going through old microfilm, looking for the lost pieces of news that would shed some light on what took place so long ago.

KILLING KATE

Thanksgiving Day 1922 was being celebrated on November 30, but it wouldn't be a day to give thanks for Kate Koopman. Cornelia Johanna Koopman, known as Kate, was having an argument with her husband, Peter. Prohibition had been in effect for two years, but Peter Koopman still had a drinking problem, moonshine being his drink of choice that evening. A former owner of the Eagle Saloon in Grand Haven, Peter Koopman's business no doubt went down the drain, along with all the liquor, after Prohibition took hold of the United States. Sometime on November 30, between 4:30 p.m. and 9 a.m. the next day, Kate Koopman was found with a bullet in her back at the foot of her staircase near the front door of the home.

Between those hours, townsfolk reported strange behavior from Peter Koopman. Peter arrived at the Bronsema & Griswald Stables in Grand Haven on Thanksgiving Day at 3:00 p.m. and asked fifteen-year-old Oscar Erhmann to make a phone call to his wife, Kate. He instructed Oscar to ask her if Peter was home. Peter also asked if Oscar would get a friend to spy on his house to see if anyone came out. Oscar made the phone call, but it's not known whether he got a friend to perform "lookout" for Peter.

Peter came back to the stables a couple hours later and asked Oscar for a ride to the Floto farm. Oscar drove Peter to the farm in his Ford truck, and Peter told Oscar not to drive past his home. The young Oscar was disturbed by Peter's erratic behavior, even more so when Peter stated, "I lost something at the Floto farm and if I don't find it, I'm going to go lay on a railroad track."

As Oscar pulled up to the Floto farm, they were greeted by Mrs. Floto, who asked Oscar to turn around and take Peter back home. It was obvious to her that Peter was drunk and irate, and she wasn't going to tolerate it. In his drunken state, Peter told Mrs. Floto that he had a gun on him. According to her statement, she took the gun out of his overcoat pocket while he was turning around to leave. While trying to escape the murder he had no doubt committed, Peter found himself at the home of Jack Buss, who later testified that Peter was incoherent, mumbling something to the effect of: "I might have shot over their heads."

Scared to go home that night, Peter passed out in the barn of John Bell at 211 Fulton, not far from his home, where his wife lay dead. Deciding that it wouldn't be a good idea to just leave him in the barn, John Bell, having no idea what was truly eating away at Peter, brought him inside their home. Peter then asked John to "walk over to his house and check on things." Bell asked his friend Jim Stone to make a quick run over there while he kept an eye of the inebriated Peter. Stone came back, reporting he had spoken with Mrs. Koopman and everything was fine. If terror wasn't already running through the frantic mind of Peter Koopman, it must have gone into overdrive after hearing that his dead wife was alive and well. Jim Stone had, in fact, just passed by the home, saw the lights on and preferred not to bother Mrs. Koopman, telling Peter she was fine to quiet him down.

The following morning, the murder of Kate Koopman was discovered, and John Bell immediately notified the police that Peter was at his home. It seemed pretty obvious to everyone what had happened. Peter was taken into custody. From the moment he viewed his dead wife, crying at the sight of her dead body and touching her cold face, Peter claimed that he knew nothing of the murder or how it happened. Was he telling the truth? Or did he kill his wife in a drunken rage that he didn't even remember? Peter refused to answer all questions asked of him from the moment of his arrest at the advice of his lawyer, Charles E. Misner.

On December 4, 1922, Kate's body was laid out in the parlor of their home for viewing, and later it was buried with her family in Lake Forest Cemetery. When the trial began, Peter was nervous, constantly moving about in his seat while the prosecutor began his questioning. When Misner took his turn, Peter relaxed. All three of Kate and Peter's kids sat in the front of the courtroom, waiting to learn what had happened to their mother and the verdict that would decide their father's fate.

During the lawyer's questioning of the jury, nearly all of the jury members were excused because they had preconceived notions about the case, had read articles in the papers and had already made up their minds about the outcome. After dismissing the entire jury and bringing in thirty new people to choose from, there was no need for them, as the trial was over the very next day. After being drawn out for months and creating one of the most sensational cases that the Ottawa County

The staircase at 310 Fulton where Kate Koopman's body was found. *Photo by Amberrose Hammond.*

Circuit Court had ever seen, Charles Misner asked for the charge of first-degree murder to be dropped. Peter offered to plead guilty of manslaughter instead. The prosecutor accepted the plea and was happy that "the many people who were witness would not have to testify in open court," especially the children. It was reported that, to spare his kids from unwanted publicity, Peter asked for the plea bargain.

When the verdict was given, the courtroom was silent. Tons of people had crammed into the courtroom to witness the trial, and the abrupt ending left people shocked. They continued to sit in the room until the court was let out for recess as if they were waiting for the prosecutor to change his mind. The verdict wasn't sitting well in the minds of the people.

Peter had spent one hundred days in the county jail before the trial started, and he didn't seem too bothered by the murder after his sentencing. The *Grand Haven Tribune* reported that visitors saw Peter the day after the trial. He was calmly playing solitaire and quickly put the cards away to welcome his guests. He admitted that he was given extra "comforts" in his cell and was well taken care of. He exercised every morning. The cell wall was scattered with pictures, one of them of his dead wife, Kate. When a reporter asked if that was his wife, no emotion flickered across his face.

The minimum time for manslaughter in 1922 was 7.5 years to a maximum of 15 years, along with a $1,000 fine. It was recommended that Peter serve the "minimum" and pay a fine of $500. Peter was officially sentenced on Friday, April 20, 1923, to Jackson Prison. He spoke "kindly of his wife" and his children and reminisced about his past with friends who came to visit him before he was shipped to Jackson.

Peter stated that his "mind had been a blank" and that he had a drinking problem but was feeling much better after having sobered up during his time in jail. The judge felt that the whole thing could have been prevented if Peter would have "stopped drinking when liquor was outlawed in the first place." An article title in the *Grand Haven Tribune* read, "Judge States Koopman's Case Should Be Warning to Others Who Follow Moonshine Trail."

After doing his time in Jackson, Peter Koopman came back to Grand Haven but seemed to be ostracized by the community for what had happened. He sold flowers from a stand to tourists to make some money and took on other small jobs. He died from a heart attack on July 19, 1949, at the age of seventy-six. His obituary doesn't mention the trial and murder of his wife, but compared to the other story titles on the *Grand Haven Tribune* page, the words "Peter Koopman Dies Suddenly" are printed in large, bold letters, making them stand out. He was buried at Lake Forest Cemetery but nowhere near Kate.

We can only speculate about what happened between Peter and Kate since Peter never admitted to killing his wife. What had they been arguing about that caused Peter to pick up a gun and pull the trigger? Did Kate know something that he didn't want her to know? Was it an argument over his drinking or his possible bootlegging of liquor during Prohibition? The truth will never be found out, but it seems that Kate might still be at her home at 310 Fulton, waiting to tell someone what happened to her so long ago in 1922.

INVESTIGATING 310 FULTON

Years went by, and no doubt many owners and people lived in the home on Fulton. At some point in the home's history, it was turned into apartments. When Linda bought the store, she spent some time restoring the home to what it used to be like and filling the rooms with clothing for her consignment shop, Second Impression. Linda had felt for some time that there was a presence in the home, and employees over the years witnessed various unexplained occurrences. A cleaning lady, who came in at night after hours, felt a presence with her one night. She stepped outside into the very small and overgrown backyard, and the light on the back of the house began to flicker. Old wiring? Perhaps. Or maybe it was a message from Kate.

A more dramatic moment involved a young girl working in the store one summer. She was sitting at the front desk when she looked up and saw a figure come down the wooden staircase directly in front of her. It was daytime, not the usual time when people expect a ghost to stop in for a visit. She was certain that she had seen a person come down the stairs, and she wasn't the type to make up stories. Another strange moment occurred after Linda had closed the shop for the day. She was almost ready to leave when she heard loud footsteps on the staircase. Thinking that someone was still in the store, she looked up at the staircase, but no one was there or anywhere else in the store.

After discovering the facts behind the murder, we conducted a simple preliminary investigation of the home and were given a tour by Linda, setting up a video camera on the stairs in the hopes that something anomalous would take place. Nothing was captured. The second time, we came back with a few more people and perched ourselves at different parts of the home. We decided to do an EVP session. EVP stands for electronic voice phenomena, and it is believed that if you ask questions or speak to the spirits, they will respond. The results sometimes show up in the recording.

A short, twenty-minute EVP session during that investigation brought about one of the most spine-tingling EVPs we had ever collected. Scott Lambert of Ghostly Talk Radio had been sitting on the top of the staircase where Linda keeps formal dresses for sale. Linda feels that Kate has always liked that area of the store; she sometimes finds that the dresses have been moved around when she opens the store in the morning. During the EVP session, we asked simple questions, such as, "Is there anyone here with us?" and "What keeps you here?" While playing the recording back at home, a part of the audio sounded different than the rest. There was a scratchy sound that didn't seem to belong with the rest of the audio levels. The recorder had been stationary and hadn't been moved around to produce the noise.

I took the sound clip and started running it through some audio programs, taking the noise down a bit, slowing the sound down, trying to figure out what was behind the strange static. As I adjusted the program and played the clip back, I wasn't ready for the voice that came through my headphones. Traditionally in the paranormal world, people don't like to front load others with what's being said in an EVP. I handed the headphones to my friend, a big tattooed guy. Big tattooed guys aren't afraid of anything, right? Jonathan ripped the headphones off and stated, "I don't want to listen to that again. That gave me goose bumps!" He had heard the very same words I had. I sent the audio clip along to the other investigators who had been there that night and asked them for their opinions on the words. They all heard the same message. It was agreed that a female voice was in the midst of the noise and sadly stated, "I'm not happy. I'm not happy. I'm not happy. Help…me." These were perfect words for someone who had been taken before her time by a bullet to the back.

But were they the words of Kate? No one can be 100 percent sure. Nothing is certain in the paranormal world; nevertheless, the results of the investigation were startling. It is sad, but the paranormal world is filled with a lot of tragedy, and tragedy seems to breed ghosts or at least paranormal phenomena. Perhaps Kate will someday find peace, or maybe she has found peace, living amongst the clothes and the shoppers who visit the store during its open hours.

IN CLOSING

If you have stories of your own to share involving tales in this book or others, please write to me. Did you grow up with a different version of a legend? Do you have a new one to tell? Share it with us! We want to hear your spooky paranormal experiences from your part of Michigan's west coast. Visit us at www.michigansotherside.com to submit your stories.

BIBLIOGRAPHY

Asfar, Dan. *Ghost Stories of Michigan.* Edmonton, MI: Ghost House Publishing, 2002.

"Beaver Island History from the Beaver Island Historical Society." http://www.beaverisland.net/history.

Bisaillon, Cindy, and Andrea Gutsche. *Mysterious Islands: Forgotten Tales of the Great Lakes.* Toronto: Lynx Images, Inc., 1999.

Bowen, Dana Thomas. *Shipwrecks of the Lakes.* Cleveland, OH: Freshwater Press, 1952.

Boyer, Dwight. *Ghost Ships of the Great Lakes.* New York: Dodd, Mead and Co., 1968.

Breisch, Kenneth A. "Hackley Public Library." *Michigan History* (May/June 1980): 35–37.

Daughters of the American Revolution. *History of Ottawa County.* Chicago: H.R. Page & Co., 1882.

Dunlop, D.S. "The Lost Treasure of Beaver Island." *Inland Seas* 43, no. 3 (1987).

Ewing, Wallace K., PhD. *Directory of Buildings & Sites in Northwest Ottawa County.* Grand Haven, MI: Tri-Cities Historical Museum, 2008.

———. *Directory of People in Northwest Ottawa County.* Grand Haven, MI: Tri-Cities Historical Museum, 2008.

Farrant, Don. "Joseph Sadony and Captain Mohr." http://spiritualteachers.org/sadony_captain_mohr.htm.

Godfrey, Linda S. *Weird Michigan.* New York: Sterling, 2006.

Haight, Louis P. *The Life of Charles Henry Hackley.* Muskegon, MI: Dana Printing Co, 1948.

Hains, Kristen M., and Earle Steele. *Beauty Is Therapy.* Traverse City, MI: Denali and Co., 2006.

Hanson, Klaus. "The Making of King Strang: A Re-Examination." *Michigan History* 46, no. 3 (1962): 201–219.

Hoyt, Susan Roark. *Lighthouses of Southwest Michigan.* Chicago: Arcadia, 2003.

Johnson, Heidi. *Angels in the Architecture.* Detroit: Wayne State University Press, 2001.

Journal of Beaver Island History 1 and 3 (1976, 1988).

Lane, Kit. *Chicora: Lost on Lake Michigan.* Douglas, MI: Pavilion Press, 1996.

McFarlane, Andrew L. "The House Under the Light." http://www.leelanau.com/nmj/summer/gt-light.html.

"The Official Joseph Sadony Website." http://www.thevalleyofthepines.com.

Oleszewski, Wes. *True Tales of Ghosts & Gales.* Gwinn, MI: Avery Color Studios, 2003.

Palmer, Richard F. "The Mormon Pirates of Beaver Island." *Insland Seas* 54 (Fall 1998): 195–198.

Price, Antje. "Protar Comes to Beaver Island." *Journal of Beaver Island* 4 (1988): 39–55.

Ratigan, William. *Great Lakes Shipwrecks & Survivals.* Grand Rapids, MI: William B. Ecrdmans Publishing Co., 1977.

Read, Frederic. *A Long Look at Muskegon.* Benton Harbor, MI: Patterson College Publications, 1976.

Rydel, Beverlee, and Kathleen Tedsen. *Haunted Travels of Michigan.* Holt, MI: Thunder Bay Press, 2008.

Sapulski, Wayne S. *Lighthouses of Lake Michigan.* Manchester, MI: Wilderness Adventure Books, 2001.

Seibold, David H. *Grand Haven: In the Path of Destiny.* Spring Lake, MI: D-2 Enterprises, 2007.

Sherman, Elizabeth B. *Beyond the Windswept Dunes: The Story of Maritime Muskegon.* Detroit: Wayne State University Press, 2003.

Stonehouse, Frederick. *Haunted Lake Michigan.* Duluth, MN: Lake Superior Port Cities Inc., 2006.

———. *Haunted Lakes.* Duluth, MN: Lake Superior Port Cities Inc., 1997.

———. *Went Missing Redux.* Gwinn, MI: Avery Color Studios, 2008.

Thomas, Henry F. *A Twentieth Century History of Allegan County.* Chicago: Lewis Publishing Company, 1907.

Widder, Keith R. *Battle for the Soul.* East Lansing: Michigan State University Press, 1999.

ABOUT THE AUTHOR

Amberrose Hammond earned her degree in English at Grand Valley State University in 2005. She has been actively researching and investigating paranormal phenomena since 2000. She has traveled around the United States and Michigan exploring haunted locations and legends and is an avid local history and historical cemetery enthusiast. She enjoys tiptoeing around old tombstones whenever she spots a new cemetery to discover. Amberrose is co-founder, along with Tom Maat, of the popular website Michigan's Otherside, which showcases Michigan's strange and paranormal world. Together, they lecture about their paranormal pursuits and enjoy sharing Michigan's mysterious side during the Halloween season with fellow Michiganders.

Photo by Kenny Biddle.

Visit us at
www.historypress.net